To Guitarist Handbook

101 Secrets to Survive, Thrive, and Succeed as a Traveling Guitarist Who Plays Live Music on the Road

HowExpert with Brandon Humphreys

For more tips related to this topic, visit www.HowExpert.com/guitar.

Recommended Resources

www.HowExpert.com – Quick 'How To' Guides on Unique Topics by Everyday Experts.

www.HowExpert.com/writers - Write About Your #1 Passion/Knowledge/Experience.

www.HowExpert.com/membership - Learn a New 'How To' Topic About Practically Everything Every Week.

www.HowExpert.com/jobs - Check Out HowExpert Jobs.

Table of Contents

Introduction

We woke up, and the world had changed. Everything was white. There was snow all over the ground in Portland, OR, and the feeling of menace was palpable in the air. It was already 9:30 am, and we'd hoped to be on the road by 9:00. I gathered my clothes and tidied up my little area of our guest apartment before making my way down to the van to put my things back in their carefully arranged spot.

The van was a rented Kia Sedona, and we were pulling a U-Haul trailer full of a our gear plus a backline of amplifiers and other gear for the headliners. There were four of us riding in it, and not a square inch of space to spare. The back of the van was filled with guitars, overnight bags, and accessory bags, and the rest of the cabin was scattered with backpacks, jackets, and other belongings. When I'd positioned myself into the rear seat, we set off. The short tour was over, and it was time to head back home.

As soon as we'd pulled out of the place we were staying, it was apparent that this was not going to be a normal drive home. Portland is a coastal city, and though it's a part of the Pacific Northwest, the city is much more accustomed to rain in the wintertime than snow. There was only about an inch and a half of accumulation, but it had brought the city to its knees.

We drove through the city streets at a snail's pace. Cars were sliding all over the roadway, and we couldn't believe what we were seeing. We knew it was going to be bad getting out of the city, but we had no idea what we were really in for. After about a half-hour and not much progress toward the highway, we decided to stop for some breakfast - maybe the weather would get a little better in an hour.

Of course, it didn't. As I sat at the counter of a charming downtown Portland diner sipping coffee and eating biscuits and gravy with my bandmates, I thought to myself, "It's gonna be a long drive home."

And boy was it. A trip from Portland back to our hometown of Spokane, WA, should normally take around six hours. By hour six of this trip, we weren't even halfway there. The storm that had dusted Portland decided to stay seated over our entire route home that day. From my viewpoint in the back passenger-side seat, I don't think I ever saw the speedometer break 45 miles per hour. Each time we would speed up to around that speed, we'd either hit a slick spot and get scared back down to around 30, or we'd see a car or two off in the ditch and decide to slow back down.

It would take a more than a few hours and many more pit stops until, in the dead of night, we pulled into our drummer's house and began to unload our gear. We were tired, irritated, and all-around shattered. We each made our way to our respective houses, and later wrote a song about the experience. That was just one of many unforgettable trips I've had as a touring guitarist.

Now, before we begin, I should say that I'm not a famous touring guitarist, and you've probably never heard of me, but I've been playing in bands on stages large and small across the western United States for the past twenty years, and I've had an amazing time doing it! Over the years, I've picked up quite a bit of knowledge, and I've learned a lot of secrets that make life easier for a guitar player on the road. This book is meant to share some of those secrets with you, so that you can get the most out of life on the road, playing in a band or on your own, as a touring guitarist.

Right off the bat, I'd like to say way to go for committing to the art of making music for other people! It's rarely as glamorous as it seems, but if you do it right, touring and playing music can be some of the most fun you can have. Even though by most standards I've never "made it big" in the music business, I've been able to check off some pretty fantastic accomplishments, and I wouldn't trade a minute of it for anything.

In this book, we'll discuss 101 secrets that can help make your time on the road that much better. We'll talk about planning a tour, promoting the tour, gear and supplies, life on the road, putting on a great show, merchandise and revenue, and networking. Whether you're a weekend warrior looking to book a couple of out-of-town shows here and there, or you're looking to embark on a coast-to-coast tour to promote your own work, this book will have something for you.

One final note before we begin: The information contained in this book is based on my experience as a touring guitarist in an original rock and roll band over the past two decades. It is not intended to endorse any specific brand or product, and any opinions expressed from here on out are my own. I hope you find this information useful, and most of all, I hope you have a great time playing music on the road.

Spreading music and sharing it with others is a noble endeavor, and I wish you the best of luck!

Chapter 1: Planning the Tour

A successful tour starts with a good plan. You need to know where you're going to play, where you're going to stay; You need figure out how to get there and how long you need between shows, and most importantly, you need open lines of communication with promoters and venue owners. This chapter will provide you with pointers and tips to help ease the planning process, and possibly help you avoid some pitfalls.

Accommodations

Tip #1: Lodging Needs

One of the first things you'll want to do when planning your tour is figure out where you're going to stay. There are a lot of options out there, and I've tried pretty close to all of them. From flying into a gig to find my gear and a hotel room key waiting for me to sleeping on some dude's lawn after a show with only five people in attendance, I've been there.

The first question you need to ask is, how many people do I need to find beds for? In many cases you will have from three to five people in the band. If you have a couple of support people touring with you, that means you'll need to plan accommodations for up to eight or more people for a small independent tour.

If it's just the band, and there are five or less, you shouldn't have too much trouble making accommodations work on a budget. If you have support people with you, it could get trickier. Most hotel room prices are based on single or double occupancy, and they may charge extra if you have extra adults checking in. So just sharing a single room is not always an option if you stick with traditional hotels or motels. On the other hand, if you're touring with a van or a large vehicle and you are traveling to a few different cities, you could take turns between staying in a room and sleeping in the van.

Tip #2: Get Creative

Let's face it, if you're starting out in the music business, and you don't have corporate sponsorship, you're going to have to be flexible in your tolerance of lodging options. In the summertime, putting up tents in a local host band's back yard can be a lot of fun. We'll talk about networking with local bands in a later chapter, but for now, keep in mind that making friends on the road can be invaluable to having a good tour. As I mentioned above, splitting the sleep-in-the-van duties is an option, though you may be able to avoid it if you're creative (I haven't had to sleep in the van for a few years now).

One of the best things to come our way in a long time is the couch-surfing industry. More than a couple of times we've used apps to book entire apartments for less than what a hotel room would cost. We've also taken to social media to ask fans in the area or friends in the area if they can help us out. In fact, the apartment I mentioned in the introduction was a guest apartment that was available for rent on a nightly basis in a friend's apartment complex. We had a whole two bedroom apartment to ourselves for about what a single occupancy room would have set us back.

Don't Forget Your Sense of Adventure!

However you do it, remember that the most important thing is making a great show happen. In my experience, some time on the road dealing with the challenges of less than perfect lodging can often make for some stellar performances.

Booking

Tip #3: Agents and Unions

If you or your band are relatively new to a scene, you might consider enlisting a local booking agent or joining the American Federation of Musicians (AFM), the national musician's union. For example, my band plays in the larger cities around the Pacific Northwest and Mountain West regions, so we have contacts in most of those cities. If we were planning a week long tour of the region and wanted to add some mid week shows in smaller towns like The Dalles, Oregon, Longview, Washington, or Moscow, Idaho, we might consider using a booking agent in any of those places since we don't have established fanbases there. Another option is to take to social media and see if there aren't some local bands in the area that you can put a show together with. We've done this a lot, and made some great contacts that way.

Dealing With Promoters and Club-Owners

There are as many horror stories out there about shady promoters and club-owners as there are audience members. And while I've certainly experienced the raw end of some deals, most of the time, as long as you act with professionalism, they will too. Communicate your needs and expectations clearly, and request clarification from them if you are unsure as to what they expect from you.

If you're unsure about a promoter or a club, talk to the other bands that have played there. One thing that I never advocate for is "pay-to-play" gigs. If you are providing entertainment and they are making money off of it, then you should be making money, too. We'll cover revenue in a later chapter, but there's no reason a decent band shouldn't be able to get paid or at least book gigs without having to pay to do so.

Tip #4: Contracts - What To Look For

Not every club owner or promoter will want to use a contract, but generally I feel better if we have one.

Remember, contracts are there to protect both parties, not just the club owner, agent, or promoter. A well-written contract can not only protect you if things go bad, they can help to prevent things from going bad in the first place.

First things first. Read Your Contract. You absolutely, positively have to read your contract. Most of the time, in my experience, the contracts one signs for most gigs are not overly complicated. A good contract should plainly specify things like what time you're expected to load in and where, what attire you're expected to wear, how long they expect you to play, what kind of songs they expect you to play, break schedules (if any), ticket information and payment arrangements, and possibly a rider.

Riders

A rider is an attachment to the contract that contains things the musician requires in order to make the show happen. There are some hilarious examples of these in rock and roll lore (brown M&Ms, anyone?), but they are actually a fairly common occurrence when playing festival shows, or other larger, organized events. The key to riders is to not be greedy. Ask for what you need, and even what you want, to a point, but don't be absurd.

Sometimes a rider is as simple as making sure there's water on the stage and a green room to change in. Other times, it can be as complicated as making sure that specific dietary requirements are met (if food is part of the deal) or that certain specialty equipment is available for use during the show (lighting, special effects, etc.) In most of my experience, our riders include water, a six pack or two of beer, some food, and a green room to use before and after our set.

Scheduling The Tour

Tip #5: Give Yourself Enough Time

It's important to understand the distances and times between shows, and to plan for delays - especially in the winter time. Snow, mechanical issues, construction, and traffic accidents are all common occurrences while on the road, and it's best to be prepared for all of them. Google Maps and other GPS apps are great for estimating driving time under ideal conditions, but life isn't always ideal.

Beyond the unfortunate incidents mentioned above, there are other considerations, too. On one of our trips, we played a late show in Missoula, Montana and pitched a tent in the yard of one of the members of the band with whom we booked the show. We didn't even get inside of our tents until close to or just after 5 am. Ordinarily that wouldn't have been too big a deal. This time, though, we happened to have booked a radio interview in Boise, Idaho early the next afternoon. We knew going in that we were going to have to leave for Boise very early in order to make our booking, but we didn't take into account how late we would probably be up the night before.

None of us were happy during the seven-and-a-half hour drive that morning, and we arrived at our hotel room in Boise with only a few minutes to freshen up before having to walk a few blocks to the radio station to give an interview that would (hopefully) make people want to come to our show that night. All any of us really wanted to do at that point was sleep, but we had to go promote the show. Make sure you give yourself enough time to get to your destination safely, with plenty of time for rest, and you won't make the same mistake we did.

Schedule Changes

Sometimes, for whatever reason, the schedule of a show or even a tour needs to change. If a show is extremely undersold, the club owner might decide it's not worth it to have the show, or the headlining band could be a no-show. There are a lot of different reasons for a show to be cancelled. If that happens, you'll want to be prepared to improvise.

I've been on shows on the road in which other bands have been added at the last minute because their other show got cancelled. They found the club through social media and reached out to the club owner to ask if they could join the show. Even if they didn't get any money for the show, they got the chance to win some fans in Salt Lake City (or wherever) and maybe even sold some merch.

Tip #6: Types of Shows

Beyond your normal club show, where there's usually a bar and a stage and a house PA system, and sometimes an all-ages area, there are several other types of shows that present unique benefits and drawbacks. From big shows like festivals and opening spots on national tours, to small charity benefit shows, the challenges and opportunities with these types of shows abound.

Charity Benefits

The best part of doing charity benefit shows is that you do great work to help out people in need. I've done benefit shows for organizations ranging from the American Cancer Society to Toys for Tots. Seeing the money that gets raised go toward helping people who need it is an amazing reward in and of itself. In addition to that, you can make a name for yourself and form great connections, and they're an opportunity to get more experience playing in front of a crowd.

If you're doing benefit shows on a tour, however, those stops will cost you extra money, so be prepared to consider those costs a donation. Because of that, it's usually not feasible to add extra stops to a tour for benefit shows, but if you're already in a city, for a paying show, adding a charity benefit show earlier in the day can be a great experience.

Competitions and Talent Shows

I'll be honest... I hate these kinds of shows. They are an open pit boiling with egos, fakery, backstabbing, and all the worst parts of humanity. Avoid them at all costs.

If you do end up booking yourself into one of these gawdawful nightmares, the only advice I can give you is to treat it just like any other show... except you may or may not get paid. In my experience, these contests have very little to do with talent or the quality of your music. Instead they are often dependent on how many tickets you sell or some other not-quite-shady provision of the contest rules. Use it as an opportunity to try and pick up a few new fans, and to sell some merch, but you'd do best not to count on any winnings from these kinds of events.

Festival Shows

These shows can be some of the most fun you'll have while on tour. The key with festivals is to be patient and be flexible. Festivals are big, complex things with a lot of moving parts, and promoters and organizers have their hands full at all times. A well-organized festival will provide you with a liasson, parking and loading instructions, gear requirements (often bands will share amps and drum kits - or "backline" - to make setup and teardown between bands easier) and other vital information. Make sure you follow the instructions you're given and be prepared to "hurry up and wait," as festival logistics often mean long periods of waiting followed by short periods of frenzied activities.

Festival shows offer a fantastic opportunity for you to promote yourself, sell merchandise, and network with other musicians and promoters. Whenever you book one of these shows, make sure you and your whole band bring your A game. Festivals will usually have a large built-in audience, but many of them have probably never heard you, so you really have to work to win them over.

Opening Spots

My favorite shows on tour are always the opening spots for national acts. Period. These shows have been some of the most exciting and best shows of my life. Most of the bands for whom I've opened are bands I listened to growing up in the '90s, so getting to meet and share a stage with them several times has been incredible.

With these types of shows you should be able to expect professionalism from the promoters and venue personnel, though I have had one such show opening up for a national act in a small city in which the venue's sound person was over an hour late and the promotion for the show was a disaster. No matter what, though, professionalism at these shows should be your goal. Make sure that you're where you need to be when you need to be there. And, of course, be prepared to play a great set so that the crowd is warmed up for the headliners!

Outdoor Shows

Playing outdoors is a different beast. The sound can be really wonky, the weather is rarely cooperative, often these shows are on improvised stages with questionable power setups, weird lighting phenomena, and of course... critters.

As far as sound goes, shows in large open areas are susceptible to wind. The wind likes to make weird noises in microphones and blow soundwaves around to play tricks on audiences and performers alike. If it looks like it's going to rain, it probably will, so you should cover the stage as much as possible to protect your gear and yourselves. Check your grounding when it comes to power. Try not to overload any circuits. It's best to have a good supply of extension cords with you if you plan on doing outdoor shows on your tour. You will also want to clean your gear after an outdoor show, as dust can wreak havoc on electronics.

Shows during the day, especially for guitar players that use pedalboards or other floor effects, can be challenging. The direct sunlight often obscures lcd displays and led on/off indicators on pedalboards, and forget about reading your tuner in the direct sunlight. I've played entire shows in the direct sunlight where I couldn't figure out why my tone was off, only to find that a pedal had been on the entire set and I couldn't tell because I couldn't see the light. Shows at night can also pose problems for lighting. If colored stage lights are the only light sources at the outdoor venue, it will be really hard to see and connect with the audience, it may also make seeing your gear difficult, depending on the setup.

A final note about outdoor shows. There will be bugs. Oh yes, there will be bugs. I've also had random pets like dogs and cats join me onstage during solos. Be prepared.

Wineries and Breweries

These shows are usually a lot of fun. They are typically smaller venues, with intimate settings. There's a lot of fun opportunities to change up your playing to match such a venue. If you're normally a loud rock and roll band, for instance, you can play more subdued versions of your songs, for instance. My band has done this in the past. For example, we've swapped an electric rhythm guitar for an acoustic, and I myself will use a smaller pedal and amp setup. It's fun for me because I get to figure out slightly different parts to play for songs that might otherwise go stale.

Tip #7: Tour Support

Managers

If you can only have one support person on your tour with you, bring a manager. As a performer, your time on the road will be so much better if there's someone else there to communicate and coordinate with club owners and promoters, sound technicians, stage managers, and the like. It is an extra bed to think about, and a cut of the revenue if you take a good one, but if you can afford it, take a manager with you.

Roadies

If there's a friend or two, or even significant others who want to tag along in exchange for helping load gear and run the merch booth while you do artist things, let them. It is usually not feasible to be able to pay people other than a manager to do this type of thing, though.

Guitar Technicians

Similar to roadies, if you have a friend who wants to come with you, and you trust that person to set up your gear for you and tune your guitars between songs, by all means do it. I have had the luxury of such a friend on two separate tours and it was amazing. Of course, the needs of the band come first, so a manager is still your best bet if you can only bring one extra person along.

Tip #8: Dos and Don'ts

Dos

Get creative and be adventurous when planning accommodations

READ YOUR CONTRACTS!

Give yourself enough time between shows

Book festival shows, opening spots, and winery/brewery shows as often as possible.

Take a tour manager if possible.

Don'ts

Don't be late.

Don't book contests or talent show competitions if you can help it.

Don't forget your sense of adventure and don't forget to be flexible.

Chapter 2: Promoting Your Tour

Now that you've planned the tour, it's time to get the word out. You want people in those seats, and you want them to be engaged. You need to pull out all the stops to make sure people know about the show. This chapter is dedicated to tips on how to promote shows in areas that are not your home market.

Writing a Press Release

Tip #9: Why Write A Press Release

The fact is, news and media editors need content. If you're worried that none of those editors are going to care that you're coming to their town, don't be. Even if you don't get any coverage in the larger papers, blogs, TV stations, or other media, you will most likely get some coverage out of smaller publications. If you're new to an area, or even if you have an established fanbase there, you want people to know you're coming. You should send out press releases to local media outlets in every town and city on your tour. This is an absolute necessity for charity benefit shows, but you should treat it as a necessity for all of your other shows too.

Tip #10: Formatting and Content

There are a lot of examples online of the proper format for a press release, so we won't spend too much time on that here, but keep in mind that the more work you do on your press release, the less work the reporter or editor is going to have to do on the story, and the more likely it is to get covered.

You need a good headline first, then address the five W's. Who are you? - Give a brief history of yourself or the band. What are you doing in their town? - Briefly mention and describe the show. Where are you playing; and When is the show? - Don't forget these important show details. Why are you playing there? - If you're doing a benefit, promoting your album, or opening for a national act, make sure you mention it.

Finally, make sure you include your contact information. A reporter, DJ, or producer may want to contact you for an interview.

Tip #11: Where to Submit

Submit your press release to every media outlet in whatever market you're traveling to. Do some research and find out about the smaller weekly periodicals that cover local events. Send them to TV producers, radio program directors, newspaper editors, and any other community events outlet you can think of. The contact information for these organizations is usually available on their websites.

Social Media Engagement

Tip #12: Facebook Events and Groups

Create a Facebook Event for every date on your tour. If you have friends or other contacts in those cities, send them direct invitations. Otherwise, you may want to set aside some money in your budget for using Facebook's promotional tours to target potential fans in those markets. You can also do some basic research online to try and find music-oriented Facebook groups in the area. You can message the moderators to see if they'll let you promote your event on their page.

Tip #13: Instagram, Periscope, and Tweets From The Road

All three of these social media formats are incredibly useful to reach out to fans while you're out on the road. For one thing, snapping pics, streaming video, and coming up with fun tweets are all great ways of killing boredom between cities. You can use Facebook Live instead of Periscope if you have a bigger fan base there. It is a good idea to look into your analytics on these social media sites. You can see when your posts get the most engagement, and schedule them to have the biggest impact.

As for what to post, pretty much anything goes as long as it's related to what's going on with the band (within bounds of taste, of course). The important thing is to get fan engagement. If you're on their minds, they're going to want to come to the show. You should at least be posting daily tour video diaries, if not a plethora of photos - band members, scenery, show pics, anything interesting. You want your posts to show up in people's feeds, and the more you post, the better the chances of that happening.

Tip #14: E-mail and RSS Feeds

You'll want to create an e-mail subscription sheet to have out at your merch booth during shows. That way, you can update new fans in each city the next time you come back, and you can also use those lists to ask fans for help with lodging or other logistical challenges when coming back to a city. You can also combine your mailing list with RSS feeds and send out updates and other tidbits periodically.

Tip #15: Reddit, Craigslist, and Other Potentially Local Forums

On Reddit, check the subreddits for the cities you're visiting first. See if they allow promotional posts, and then post away. For example, if I were playing in Denver, I would first visit r/Denver and see if I could post the press release I wrote for the show there. If the moderators wouldn't allow a post like that, I'd ask them via direct message if they could point me to a subreddit that would be more appropriate. In any case, it doesn't take too long and Reddit can be a great place to promote your show.

Local Craigslist boards will most likely have forums where you can advertise or post your press release. You can also use Google to find other local forums on which you can promote the show. Again, these are things you can be doing on your phone in the van (if you're not driving) while getting to the first or next stop on your tour if you don't have time to do it beforehand.

Tip #16: YouTube

If you've got a manager, roadies, or other support personnel on tour with you, have them record as much footage of the shows as possible so that you can edit videos for YouTube. Whether you decide to post entire songs, or just a compilation with snippets of each song, having a video of current live footage available for potential fans to look at is very important. If you didn't bring any support personnel with you, see if you can have the sound technician or club owner press record on your phone for you. In fact, a good item to purchase before you hit the road is a portable cell-phone tripod. I have one that will wrap around almost any object. I also have a bluetooth controller for the camera on my phone. With these items, even if you can't find anyone to help you record, you can do it yourself from the stage.

Radio Promotion

Tip #17: Getting Air Time

Your best option for getting air time if you don't have any radio contacts in the market is to use your press release. Do a little research beforehand and send your press release to the program director, or the local spotlight host (sometimes stations will do programming blocks highlighting local events). It may be difficult if you don't have any contacts in the market to get air time on a major station, since most stations these days are owned by giant media conglomerates. In this case, check with local college stations or public and community radio stations. Any air time you can get will help.

Tip #18: Interviews

First of all, bring an acoustic guitar with you. Period. I'll cover a lot of things about gear in the next chapter, but for now, know that one of the many uses for an acoustic guitar on the road is that radio stations - especially the public and community owned ones (who may actually still do live radio) - will probably want you to play something acoustic in-studio for the spot. Even if you're in a metal band, bring an acoustic so you can play something on the air to help get fans to the show.

Second, when it comes to interviews, it's a good idea to think of what you're going to say before you get the mic in front of you. If you're in a band, have a

discussion with your bandmates about what you do
and don't want fans to know. If you're a solo act, you
don't want to freeze up when the interviewer asks you
a question. Common things brought up in interviews
include where you're from, how your band formed,
who your musical influences are, and what your future
plans are. If you make sure you have answers for
those questions, you should be good to go.

Tip #19: Local Periodicals

Most cities will have one or more weekly periodicals
that highlight local events like concerts, sports, etc.
Make sure these publications are on your mailing list
for your press release. They may already be printing
up a byline that the venue owner has sent them, but if
you send them a press release with a good band photo
you may get a featured spot.

Photo Shoots

It's a good idea to include some quality band photos
with your press release when contacting the editors of
these periodicals. It adds an air of professionalism
and helps them put a personality to the press release.
Having your buddy take some photos with his or her
iPhone is okay, but it's a better idea if you can afford it
to pay a photographer for some quality photos where
the lighting is good. Live performance shots are also
good, provided they are of sufficient quality.

Posters and Flyers

Tip #20: Printing Tips

Whether you go with one show poster design for your entire tour, or you decide to do a different poster for each city, having some actual paper posters up around town can really help. Check Yelp and other customer review sites to find local printers. You can work with the promoter or the venue owner to have them pick up and distribute posters or flyers, or you can recruit a street team.

Tip #21: Street Teams

If you already have some fans in the area, send out an e-mail or some social media posts asking for street team volunteers. Street teams are groups of volunteers that go out on the streets of a city you're planning on visiting and distribute flyers and posters. If you don't know anyone local, you can try offering free tickets to the show for volunteers via local bulletin boards or subreddits.

Chapter 3: Gear and Supplies

Having the right gear and taking care of it is essential
for putting on a good show. Now, don't get me wrong,
"having the right gear" doesn't necessarily mean
having the most gear or having the most expensive
gear. What it means is having the tools necessary to
play a great set. In this chapter, we'll discuss
everything gear related - from the large ticket items to
the life-saving accessories that are so easy to overlook.
For each category, I'll do my best to give advice on
how to build a quality touring setup regardless of your
budget, and offer suggestions about taking care of that
gear in the face of the punishment the road will put it
through.

Acoustic Guitars

As a general rule, in addition to considering sound,
playability, and looks, you want to take guitars with
you that are durable and versatile. This is especially
true of acoustic guitars. When trying to decide which
guitar(s) to bring on tour, you'll want to think about
amplification options, feedback control, and wood
characteristics.

Tip #22: Amplification Options

Amplifying acoustic guitars can be a tricky business.
Audio purists will often prefer a condenser

microphone placed on a stand in front of the guitar, as that is perhaps the most faithful way to capture the real sound of the guitar. In many cases, however, this adds complication to setup and teardown, and it can become incredibly difficult to control feedback with such setups if the sound technician doesn't know what he or she is doing. On the other hand, piezoelectric (or transducer) pickups, often have a tinny, artificial sound that is downright offensive to those who truly appreciate the tone of an acoustic guitar, though the higher-end systems are able to mitigate this issue somewhat with the use of active EQ circuitry.

A good compromise is a system that uses a blend of both a piezoelectric pickup and a condenser microphone. These systems will often have a small condenser microphone installed in the body of the guitar, and use that input with a piezoelectric pickup under the saddle to create a hybrid signal to send to the sound board or amplifier.

Another option if you don't have a pickup in your guitar, and if you don't want the hassle of a microphone setup on stage, is a slide-in style magnetic pickup. These pickups are inexpensive and work just like an electric guitar's magnetic pickups. They slide into the sound hole for easy on/off installation, though sometimes they can be more permanently mounted. Sound-wise, some people say these pickups outperform either of the options mentioned above.

As far as the actual amplification source, unless you really love the tone of a standalone acoustic guitar amplifier, you'll probably just want to use a direct box (see the section on these later) and plug straight into the PA system.

A Note About Wood and Tone

If you're new to playing acoustic guitar, you may not realize that the type of wood acoustic guitars are made of can have a big effect on their tonal characteristics. For the most part, the wood on the top of the guitar is going to have the biggest effect on the overall tone. For that reason, most players will prefer a "solid" top, meaning that it's a full piece of wood rather than a laminate or composite. Solid tops will age and their tonal characteristics will change over time. They're also more susceptible to humidity and temperature changes. Because of this, you may want to consider taking a laminate top acoustic with a good pickup system over that beautiful vintage solid-top Martin in grandpa's closet. On stage in a club or large venue, the solid top in grandpa's Martin won't make as much of a difference in tone as the electronics will. That said, if you do end up choosing a solid top guitar, here are some things to note.

Spruce vs. Cedar

The two most common woods found on the top of acoustic guitars are spruce and cedar. Generally speaking, spruce has a brighter, more trebly tone, while cedar is warmer and more bassy. If you're unsure about which wood you're looking at, spruce is usually a lighter shade while cedar is darker. Of course, if your guitar has an opaque or colored finish, you won't be able to tell by looking at it.

Amplifiers

If you're an electric guitar player, the amplifier is the beating, bleeding heart of your tone. You want an amp that is powerful enough to fill a hall, but delicate enough to be able to use in an intimate setting like a winery or a brewery. You want an amp that sounds great in any situation, so versatility is key. There are a lot of choices out there, from clean tube amp combos to gigantic high-gain stacks. This section will help you to break down which amplifier to bring and which to leave home.

Tip #23: Tube vs. Solid State/Modeling

"Tube" amps are those amps which are powered by a series of vacuum tubes (similar to those in old radio equipment before the invention of the transistor). A true tube amp will have two sets of tubes - a pre-amp section, and a power-amp section. The pre-amp is the part of the amplifier that processes the raw signal from the guitar before it hits the amplification circuit. The power-amp is the part that actually amplifies the signal from a weak line level signal, to the high-wattage signal that's sent to the speaker. The types of tubes used in each section will vary greatly by manufacturer and model, as will the tone.

Tube amps have a reputation for being temperamental, and to be honest, they kind of are if you compare them to solid-state amps. With solid-state amps, you don't have to replace tubes, you will most likely not blow a fuse, and they're not nearly as susceptible to humidity, temperature, and motion. That said, they are lifeless, soulless shells of what an amplifier should be. I've yet to come across a solid state amp that even comes close to the tone of any tube amp I've ever played. Don't waste your time with solid state. Buy and bring a tube amp...

...Unless you plan on using a modeling setup (by "modeling" I mean a processing system like those in the Line 6 POD). Some guitarists out there swear by modern software processing power, and I can't really say I blame them. In fact, on the second tour I ever did, I toured with only a Line 6 POD and the accompanying floorboard. I plugged directly into the PA system at every gig - even at a large festival gig with a couple of thousand people in the audience. The sound guy there looked at me a little funny, until he checked my levels and heard the tone, then he was all smiles.

If you do plan on using modeling, I suggest you do things that way rather than buying a modeling amp. To me, a modeling amp misses out on the best part of modeling technology - realistic amplifier tone without having to actually carry an amp around.

One final note about tube vs. solid state technology - Tube watts are louder than solid state watts. I know this seems ridiculous, but trust me, it's true. If you put a 60W tube amp next to a 100W solid state amp, the tube amp will kill your eardrums well before the solid state one will. If you're looking for a tube amp, chances are you'll never need anything louder than a 60W power output. In fact, for a lot of shows, my 15W Vox AC15C Combo is more than powerful enough.

Tip #24: Combo vs. Head & Cabinet

As you might have been able to tell already, I don't like a big hassle during setup and tear-down, and I hate carrying more gear than I need to into a venue. So, of course, I'm going to be biased in this category toward combos. I have toured exclusively with combos, with the exception of the one tour mentioned above in which I used a Line 6 POD direct into the board, with no amplifier at all. Nevertheless, I recognize that there are those guitarists for whom rock & roll just isn't rock & roll without at least a Marshall half-stack. So let's go over the basics, shall we?

"Combo" refers to amplifier setups in which the "head" - or the amplifier itself - is housed within the same (typically wood) enclosure as the speaker(s). The common speaker configurations for combos are 1X12", 2X12", and 4X10". Combos will usually range from 15W ~ 60W as far as power goes. The advantage of touring with a combo amp is that they are relatively easy to move around and take up less space than a head/cabinet setup.

"Head & Cabinet" refers to setups in which the amplifier, or "head," is housed in a separate chassis from the speaker cabinet. In general, this adds versatility to an amplifier because the speaker configuration can have a big impact on the tone. For example, a 60W combo amp that has a 1X12 speaker will sound weaker than the same amplifier head powering a 2x12 or a 4X12 speaker cabinet. The amp is not actually delivering more power, but the speakers themselves are pushing a larger volume of air, so the sound is more full.

Tip #25: Microphone Placement vs. Line Out

Unless you're planning on using a modeling setup (i.e. Line 6 POD, etc.), you may just want to forget that jack on the back of the amplifier that says "line out." What this jack does is send a "line" level signal out to another amplifier, like a PA system. Unfortunately, the line level signal doesn't include your power tubes or other integral parts of the amplifier circuit, so the tone is usually terrible. Just don't use it.

Instead, nearly all guitar amplifiers, once they get on stage, will have a microphone placed in front of the speaker. In the case of speaker cabinets or combos with multiple speakers, only one speaker is usually mic'd up. For this reason, I prefer to tour with a 1X12 combo amp. The extra speakers are not going to go through the PA, so the only people who will notice the difference between one speaker and four speakers will be the ones standing close to the amps. The rest of the audience won't hear a difference.

When placing the microphone in front of the speaker, there are several common placement options from which to choose. Some guitarists like the microphone to be pressed right up against the grill cloth, while others like it an inch or two away. There's also the question of whether to position the microphone so that it's pointed right at the speaker cone (the center of the speaker) or if it's pointed at the edge of the speaker, and whether the mic will be pointed straight, or on an axis. There's no real "right" way to do it, since tone is so subjective. Your best bet is to play around with different placements and see which one you like best.

Tip #26: Common Settings

With a few variations, most amplifiers will have the same basic controls. Depending on how the amp is designed, there may be multiple channels with multiple controls for each channel. The main controls you need to be concerned with are for volume, gain, EQ, and effects.

As far as volume goes, there are often a couple of different controls that will affect the overall volume of the amplifier. These are usually labeled either "level," "gain," or "drive." In tube amps, these controls are differentiated by which part of the amp they affect. Typically "level" controls the output level of the power amp, and has the biggest effect on the volume of the amp. On some amps, there will be a level setting for each channel, and a master level setting as well. On these types of amps, there may not be a separate control for gain or drive. Instead, to achieve an overdrive sound on these amps, you would typically want to increase your output level on the channel, and use the master level to control overall volume.

Regarding EQ, each amp will respond differently to these controls. Some amps sound best when you have the bass and treble at a moderate level and the mids cranked, while other amps sound best with the bass and treble raised and the mids scooped out. For the most part, once you find a tone you like, you should keep those settings, however sometimes a different room will require some EQ or gain adjustment.

If an amp has a specified gain control or a high-gain channel (for getting a distorted tone), you'll want to dial this in rather than just cranking it to eleven. Sorry, Spinal Tap fans. Believe it or not, you can have way too much gain, and it can kill your tone. As a rule, I try not to go above 70% on the gain knob. If I want a higher-gain sound, I use a Big Muff or other distortion pedal (see the effects section later on in this chapter). The point is, play around with the gain channel and find a setting you like instead of just cranking it.

Tip #27: Troubleshooting and Maintenance

For the tour, you should find out what kind of fuses your amp needs and bring a couple of spares. You should also bring an extra set of power tubes (preamp tubes almost never need to be replaced). Power tubes need to be biased together in pairs, so make sure you get a matched set.

You can find detailed instructions online for replacing tubes, but if you're nervous about doing it, you should try it at home before you get out on the road and have to do it twenty minutes before showtime. You don't need to be a certified repair technician to change power tubes on most amps. It's a relatively simple procedure, but this book is not intended to be a service guide, so you should definitely watch an instructional video from a trusted source online, or read the manual first. There are some important safety steps that you'll want to observe beforehand.

The last bit to consider with maintaining or troubleshooting your amp is the speaker cable. The speaker cable is a cable that runs from the amplifier head to the speaker cabinet; however, even on combo amps there is a speaker cable that runs from the chassis of the amplifier to the speaker itself. These cables can and will go bad. Bring a spare... or two.

Tip #28: Cables

Yes, Your Cables Matter.

I was once told by a U.S. Air Force tech school instructor that when it comes to diagnosing problems with electronics, 70% of the time, it's a cable. Anecdotally I have found this to be true. Cables are the viaduct through which the water of your tone flows. If you buy cheap cables, you should buy a lot of them.

On the other hand, if you invest more money up front on high quality guitar and speaker cables, you won't spend nearly as much in the long run. I used to be a non-believer, but I have seen... er... heard the light, and I can tell you, your cables matter. Apart from breaking less often, high quality cables do, in fact, sound better. As I said, I used to think the idea was ridiculous, but I decided to put it to the test myself. I set up an auditory experiment in which I played the same same riff on the same guitar plugged directly into the same amplifier twice and recorded it each time. I used the same microphone and the same recording software. The only variable was the instrument cable. I listened to each recording in an A/B comparison, and I can tell you it was like someone removing a foam board from the front of my amp when I heard the quality cable after the cheap one. I have since replaced every cable in my rig with that particular brand, and I have only had to replace one of them (which the company did for free, by the way) when it went bad after at least a couple of years of hard service on the road.

Distance and Impedance

This book is not meant to get into too much technical detail, but we should say a word or two about impedance. Impedance is the measure of resistance on an electrical signal, and it is measured in Ohms.

There are two ways, in general, that impedance affects your gear. First, if you have a lot of pedals and a lot of cable length, your tone will be weaker when it gets to the amp than if you just plug directly in. That being said, if you plug directly in with a 25' cable, your tone will be weaker than if you plug in with a 10' cable. In short, the longer the cable or signal chain between your guitar and the amp, the weaker your signal will be because of the high-impedance nature of guitar cables. So unless you absolutely need to run to the other side of the venue to play your solo, try to keep your cable distances to a minimum.

The other way impedance can affect you is when matching speaker cabinets to amplifier heads. You want to make sure the impedance rating matches. For example, if your amplifier puts out 60 Watt at 8 Ohms, you want to plug it into an 8 Ohm speaker cabinet. Higher or lower impedance loads can damage your amplifier or the speakers themselves, so make sure the ratings match.

Tip #29: Capos

If you use a capo, make sure you bring a quality one on the road with you. There are quality options in a couple of different designs. The spring-operated design offers quick changeovers between songs, but sometimes tuning can suffer on higher frets. The other option is the lever-operated design. If you don't change capo positions a lot between songs I recommend this design because it has a screw in the back that adjusts the pressure on the strings, thereby saving tuning stability.

Tip #30: Direct Boxes

When you want to use an acoustic guitar that has a pickup, it's usually not practical to plug a cable directly from your guitar into the sound board. For one thing, the board is often at the back of the venue, and for another thing, the board is usually set up to accept low-impedance XLR-style microphone cables, not high-impedance guitar cables. Because of this, you'll want to use a direct box. This handy little box takes the high-impedance signal from your guitar and turns it into a low-impedance signal for the sound board.

Effects

Effects, when used properly, can really help you and your playing stand out from the other bands. They can also kill your show if they're mishandled. I'll do my best here to explain the most common types of effects and how to set them up so they accentuate your playing rather than detracting from it.

Tip #31: Signal Chain

Whether you're using a multi-effects processor or an old-fashioned pedalboard, the order in which the effects are added to the signal is extremely important in shaping your tone. Generally speaking you want miscellaneous effects like wah, compression, and pitch-shifting effects to go first. After that, you'll want to place your gain effects, i.e. distortion or fuzz. Next should go any modulation effects such as chorus or tremolo. Finally, delay and reverb effects should be last in the chain.

Tip #32: Compression, Wah, and Pitch Shift

Compressors are a very useful tool. Their job is to remove the extreme peaks and valleys from your signal, thereby "compressing" it. Sonically, this results in a nice, smooth tone for guitar players. If you overuse compression, though, you'll lose some of the dynamic quality to your playing, so make sure you keep it tasteful. Compression is used a lot in country twang tones, because with a high "attack" setting, it makes the tone really crisp and sharp, and adds a sort of "spank" to it.

Wah pedals are not a crutch. Say it with me: "Wah pedals are not a crutch." Contrary to the example set by certain nineties heavy-metal and grunge icons, your foot is allowed to leave the wah pedal. In fact, you don't even have to use the wah pedal most of the time. I know, it's hard to hear, but it's true. I have a vintage-style wah pedal, which I use sparingly.

Pitch shifting effects are those created by either a Whammy pedal, octave pedal, or other pitch-shifter. They are best used sparingly, but they can be very, very cool in the right songs.

Tip #33: Distortion, Fuzz, and Overdrive

In many rock and pop settings, the overdriven, distorted, or fuzz effect makes up the bulk of the tone's character. These pedals are designed to overload the preamp section of your amp, resulting in a distorted signal. Just like with the gain setting on your amp, these pedals need to be fine tuned rather than cranked. You should experiment with them to get the sound you like.

Distortion pedals create a smooth and saturated overdrive sound. They help to recreate the tone of a high-gain amplifier and are often used for lead tones, or for hard-rock rhythms. Examples of classic distortion pedals are the RAT, the Boss DS-1, and the Electro Harmonix Big Muff.

Fuzz pedals overload the signal even more than distortion pedals do, to the point that it "clips" or breaks up too much. Because of the clipping, the tone is often much more bass-heavy than a classic distortion pedal. This makes them too muddy unsuitable for many heavy-metal or hard-rock applications. Fuzz is typically used in lead and rhythm tones for classic rock, grunge, funk, and R&B settings. Examples of classic fuzz pedals are the Dallas-Arbiter and Dunlop "Fuzz Face" models.

Overdrive pedals have a wide range of character depending on the model. For the most part, they provide less gain than distortion or fuzz pedals, but they are much more versatile. They are used in blues, country, funk, jazz, reggae, rock, R&B, soul, and just about every other style in between. For blues, country, and jazz, you will typically want to use lower-gain settings, while rock, soul, and funk will probably require higher-gain settings. Examples of popular overdrive pedals are the Ibanez Tube Screamer, Boss Blues Driver, and the Fulltone OCD.

Tip #34: Modulation Effects

Modulation effects alter the signal by modulating, or shifting, the signal in and out of phase in some way. Since this is by far the broadest category of effects, I'll just give a basic description here of the modulation effects I use on a regular basis.

Chorus

Chorus is a very versatile effect that can be used as a stand-in for both flanger and rotary effects if set properly. It's effect is typically described as sparkly or watery, and it was often used on guitars in the 1980s.

There are many models on the market, though I typically prefer the analog variety.

Phaser

Phaser shifts the phase of the sine wave (signal) in either two or four stages. It creates a very fluid in-and-out sound, and is widely used on guitar solos from the 1970s and '80s to add color to the tone. Some common examples of phasers are the MXR Phase 90 and the Electro-Harmonix Small Stone.

Rotary

This is one of my favorite effects to use, but it's not quite as popular as some of the other modulation categories. It simulates the effect of a rotating speaker cabinet, creating the "doppler effect," which is often described as sounding "underwater," It is similar to a chorus effect, but it is more pronounced and distinct. Two examples of rotary simulators are the Boss RT-20 and the Dunlop Rotovibe.

Uni-Vibe

The Uni-Vibe was a unique phaser/chorus effect originally produced in the 1960s. It was made popular by guitarists like Jimi Hendrix and Robin Trower. It is technically a phase shifter, though it's wide range of controls makes it useful as a rotary simulator as well. The original Uni-Vibe units are collector's items these days, but there are many clones out there, namely the Fulltone Deja-Vibe.

Tremolo

Tremolo is a necessity for my style of music. There are several different types out there, but usually if you have a Fender or Vox tube amp you'll have some type of tremolo on it. If not, there are some great stomp-box options available. Many of them will let you choose the type of wave you want – sine $\sim$, or square $\sqcap$. This determines how soft or hard the tremolo effect is. Some tremolo units also have a feature that will change the speed and intensity of the effect based on how hard you play. If you play blues, country, surf, or classic rock, tremolo is a must for you.

Vibrato

Vibrato comes standard on a lot of Fender tube amps, and is a very similar effect to tremolo, though the sound is always a sine wave and is softer than tremolo. If your amp doesn't have vibrato on it, it's probably a better idea to just achieve this effect with either a chorus pedal (set the speed and depth controls to high levels) or tremolo (use a sine wave setting and turn the intensity down).

Filters

Many funk players like to use envelope and other modulating filters. These filters change the tone and the modulation to create synth-like tones or even an auto-wah effect. There are a lot of different kinds of filters out there, so be sure you try them out before buying one for your pedalboard, though.

Tip #35: Delay, Echo, and Reverb

Rather than changing the tone or modulation of your signal, the delay pedal takes a snapshot of your notes and then repeats that snapshot however you want it to be repeated. The easiest way to think of this family of effects is to think of them all as "echo" effects, meaning they're using repetition of the signal at time intervals to create the effect.

Delay

Delay can be either digital or analog. It differs from effects that are marketed as "echo" effects in that delay usually allows for a wider range of time options. Most delay pedals and processors, if they don't have a tap tempo feature, will measure the rhythm of the delay in milliseconds. for example a fairly quick delay will be in the 0-200ms range, while medium is usually 200-600ms, and long is 600ms and up. Some units will allow you to set a tempo by tapping, and other, even smarter units will allow you to divide the tempo you set by note type - whole, half, quarter, dotted quarter, eighth, dotted eighth, and even more.

Feedback on a delay pedal controls the number of times the signal repeats. The higher the setting, the more repeats you get. A lot of units will also have a mix, wet/dry, or effects level control. This will help you control the mix between the dry signal and the delay.

Many units will advertise stereo delay as a feature. Unless you plan on lugging two amps around or plugging directly into two channels of the mixer board, this is useless to you in a live setting. You can't use stereo delay any other way. That feature is mostly for recording. There may be many other fun features on your delay unit though, so make sure to spend some time with the manual and get the most out of it.

One of the most common settings in pop music has been made popular by the likes of The Edge from U2 and David Gilmore from Pink Floyd on songs like "Where the Streets Have No Names," "I Still Haven't Found What I'm Looking For," "Another Brick in the Wall, Pt. 1" and "Run Like Hell," respectively. The easiest way to achieve this effect is with a tap tempo and the dotted-eighth-note setting. Tap in the tempo of the song in quarter notes, then play muted eighth notes. It creates a very unique delay rhythm.

Echo

Typically, if an effects unit is being advertised as "echo," it means it's going to have a fairly short time range (0-400ms) and not a lot of options for feedback (number of repetitions). It's intended to be a vintage style effect mimicking the early tube amps and tube echo units.

Reverb

Reverb is tricky. It's a cool effect, to be sure. Especially on a record. Live, however, you can shoot yourself in the foot with it very easily. The point of reverb is to make it sound like your guitar is being played in a specific physical environment, or room. If you want it to sound like you're in a tile bathroom, then you would set the reverb to be a very short slapback or something like that. On the other hand, if you want it to sound like you're in a gymnasium or a concert hall, you would want to turn the reverb up a bit.

The problem, then, is that when you're playing live, you're already in a physical environment which will undoubtedly have its own acoustic properties. In other words, the room is going to have its own natural reverb. Chances are, if you add more, it's going to muddy up your tone. Even in small clubs packed with people there is a decent amount of natural reverb. So for me, on the road, the reverb is always off unless I'm specifically trying to drench the signal for a surf tune or something like that.

If you use the reverb on your amp, then you will have relatively few controls to worry about. If you use a separate effects unit, you will have a lot of controls like decay, attack, tone, etc. You'll want to set these to the room if you plan on using the reverb for a specific effect. Remember: The consequences of over-doing reverb are grim. Your tone will be muddy and get eaten up in its own gluttony. If the sound guy tries to drench your tone in reverb, flog him (okay, don't flog him, but feel free to give him a firm talking to and remind him that it's not 1982 anymore).

Tip #36: Effects Loops

Many amplifiers have an effects loop feature. This allows you to insert your effects into the power amplifier directly, which means that your guitar signal travels through the amp's preamp stage first. These systems were first designed for rack-mounted effects units, but they are also useful with delay and reverb effects pedals. Most other types of pedals (distortion, modulation, etc) are designed to be plugged directly into the amplifier's input, and sound better that way.

One other advantage of some modern effects loops is that they have separate level controls for input and output, which means you can shape the tone more. It also, however, means that you can actually use the effects loop of your amp as a lead boost! This is what I do with my Fender amp. You simply run a short patch cable from the effects loop input to the effects loop output and use the level controls to change the output level when the effects loop circuit is activated (usually via footswitch). This way, the only thing the effects loop is doing is raising the volume level of the signal.

Footswitches

When choosing an amplifier, you may want to consider what kind of footswitch is available with it. Many amps have a few different options. If you have an amp with more than one channel (i.e. clean and gain), you will want to make sure you have a footswitch to change between them. Additionally, a footswitch may have controls to switch gain levels, turn on reverb/tremolo/vibrato, or turn the effects loop on and off.

Tip #37: Grounding

When using a lot of pedals or old amplifiers, it can be easy to run into grounding issues. Grounding can also be an issue with older venues whose electricity may not be up to code (BE CAREFUL!). The most common and relatively benign symptom of bad grounding will be a nasty hum that goes away when you touch your strings or a microphone. That is the **best**-case scenario with grounding problems.

Worse case? You could get badly injured by electrical shock when you touch your strings or a microphone. If you're playing an acoustic or a bass, you will probably be using a direct box, which should have a "ground lift" feature that will help. The best way to protect yourself, though, is to run your gear a power conditioner, which we will discuss later in this chapter.

Tip #38: Guitar Care on the Road

Proper Cases

There's a reason "gig bags" are named so. They're meant for one-night stands. Take them to the show, take them home that same night, no big deal. They add enough protection for that. For an extended trip though, I definitely recommend a hard-shell case. For driving, the suitcase-style hard-cases are fine and will hold up well. For flights, though, you absolutely positively need an FAA approved case. Make sure that the lock you choose for it is TSA approved, as well.

Temperature Control

Beware when traveling through northern or desert climates where the temperature and humidity can swing wildly between extremes. If your guitars have been in a freezing trailer all day and you bring them into a heated theater or club, give them some time to acclimate before fully opening the cases. A trick I use is to crack the case just a bit and let a little warm air in, then I gently let the lid back down. Let it sit there for a few minutes, then it should be okay.

Sudden changes in temperature can be torture on your instruments. Wood does not like it at all, and will swell and contract sometimes to the extreme in reaction. Rapid temperature change can cause neck warping, finish cracks, condensation buildup and rust or corrosion in the electronics, just to name a few. This is another reason why having a good hard case is a necessity. The insulation it adds helps to keep the your guitar at a constant temperature, avoiding those nasty outcomes.

Neck Issues (Guitars)

Despite your best efforts to maintain temperature consistency, however, you may run into some issues with your neck. Commonly, a truss-rod adjustment will be in order. Either the wood will be bowing concave (in which case you need to tighten the truss-rod), or the wood will be bowing convex (in which case you would loosen the truss-rod).

The truss-rod is an adjustable metal rod that runs through the neck to keep it straight in the face of the mammoth tension placed on it by the strings. It is usually adjusted with a hex-head wrench via an access port on the headstock. This port, on Gibson, PRS, and Ibanez guitars is covered by a plastic piece. On Fenders, the port is usually open. Some manufacturers put the truss rod adjustment mechanism at the other end of the neck, which may make it more difficult to adjust right before a show.

Tip #39: New Strings

Change your strings a day or two before the tour starts. If you've got the budget and a tech with you, change them every day after that. If you don't have a tech, once a week should be okay for a tour. New strings are brighter and clearer sounding, but they do require a bit of break in. If you are going to change your strings every day, make sure you properly stretch them out before showtime.

To change strings on a standard Fender-style headstock with six in-line normal modern tuning pegs, you want to start by winding the string in a counter-clockwise direction from the bottom of the peg. I typically wind the 1st string five times before running it through the hole and clipping it. I clip my strings about a half inch from the tuning peg, and then bend the excess down. Then I wind the 2nd string four times, the 3rd three times, the 4th and 5th strings twice, and the 6th once, and repeat the clipping procedure.

With "vintage" style Fender tuners, you need to clip the string first, about three inches past the tuning peg, then stick it into the vertical hole at the top of the tuning peg and wind it counter-clockwise around the peg. You should be able to keep the same number of winds with these tuners, but they may vary.

Locking tuners require no winding. Simply feed the string through the hole in the tuning peg and tighten the locking mechanism.

If you use a dual-locking tremolo system, changing strings is a lot bigger ordeal and I feel for you. You must cut the ball end of the string off, lock it into the bridge, then execute the winding procedure I outlined above, stretch the strings, tune up, adjust the tremolo, tune up again, adjust the tremolo again, tune up again... then finally lock the nut down.

For double-sided headstocks, follow the same procedures outlined for the in-line style, but the strings will need to be wound clockwise for the bottom three tuning machines (strings 1, 2, and 3).

After you've replaced the strings, you'll need to stretch them out. This is because metal is flexible and under tension it will stretch on its own. When the strings stretch, the tension on them decreases, and the tuning goes flat. It's better to pre-stretch your strings before a show, so that they won't stretch by themselves in the middle of your solo and go horribly, horribly out of tune. I like to take a polish cloth between my thumb and index finger to pad the fingers from the string cutting into them while I stretch them. Be careful to stretch them hard, but not too hard. Too much tension will break them.

Polish

It's a good idea to polish your guitar before each show. It looks more professional and will help the finish of your guitar stay beautiful for a long time. Pretty much any guitar polish will work. Some players like to use carnauba wax or other abrasives, but those can be difficult to apply on the road. For the tour, a simple spray bottle should suffice. String cleaner can also help to keep your strings sounding new longer.

Tip #40: Pots and Jacks

Occasionally the electrical controls and connections for your guitar will become corroded and start to crackle or cut out in certain positions. When this happens, it can usually be fixed by spraying some electronics cleaner directly onto the pot post (underneath the volume or tone knob) and turning it back and forth a few times. Jacks should have their connections inspected for frayed wiring or bad solder connections. Repairing this may be more difficult, but it can be done in a pinch if you know how to solder.

Tip #41: Strap Buttons and Strap Locks

If you play out long enough, it's inevitable that you will have a strap come unfastened at some point or other. It can be mildly annoying or disastrous, depending on when and where it happens, so let's look at how to prevent it. The first thing to do is install a good set of strap locks on your guitar. To do this, simply unscrew the existing strap buttons and replace them with a set of strap-lock buttons. Next, you'll need to install the locking portion of the strap lock system onto your strap. Each style of strap lock will have a different procedure for this, so be sure to read the manufacturer's instructions. Once complete, the system should ensure that your strap stays locked onto the buttons on your guitar.

But what if those buttons come loose? That happens more than you think. Especially with guitars that have been on the road a long time. Typically what happens is that the hole into which the strap button is screwed will be bored out over time by use. When this happens, the easiest way to fix it is to remove the strap button, break off a toothpick inside the hole, and re-screw the strap button back in. The toothpick is soft, so it will fill the extra space bored out by wear and tear and help keep the button fastened to the body.

Tip #42: Other Gear Care

The most common problems with amplifiers on the road are blown fuses and blown tubes. As I mentioned earlier in this chapter, bring spares of both. Either of these issues can theoretically be fixed before a show, but tubes may take a while to break in and reach their full tonal potential.

Pedals may need to have electrical cleaner sprayed into pots and jacks to keep them in good working order. Any further repair, though, should probably not be attempted on the road.

If you get into a jam, you can check to see if another band on the bill has gear you can borrow for your set, or you can also try to find an open music store that may be able to help you out.

Pedalboards

If you're like most guitar players, you'll want at least a few of the pedals described in the effects section on tour with you. The easiest way to manage multiple pedals is to install them onto a pedalboard.

Now, a pedalboard doesn't have to be super-expensive to be effective. Heck, it doesn't even necessarily have to start out as a pedalboard. In fact, a famous musician friend of mine who tours all over the U.S. with his hit 90's band uses nothing more than a rolled-up strip of industrial Velcro. Seriously. He has about six or seven nano-sized pedals chained together with short patch cables and attached to a strip of Velcro about two feet long and a couple of inches wide. When he sets up, he just rolls it out, plugs in the power and guitar cables, and he's ready to go. Then when his set is over, he just rolls it right back up again and puts it back in his bag.

My pedalboard is the opposite extreme. It was custom made and hard-wired, and it has an extremely durable flight case for it. It's also incredibly heavy, large, and cumbersome. On the other hand, it has every pedal I use on it, hardwired and protected, and it's still as easy to set up. Just put it on the ground and plug it in.

You'll probably want something in between.

Tip #43: Designing a Pedalboard

Physical vs. Logical: There are two layers of setup that need to be considered when designing a pedalboard – the physical setup and the logical (or signal) setup. The physical layer is the way that your pedals are figuratively laid out on the board. This is important to consider because space is precious and you want to be able to fit as many pedals into as small a space as possible. Take the time to use some graph paper or an app to design the physical layout before you start buying anything.

The logical layout is the signal chain (see above), or the path that the guitar signal takes through the pedals. Sometimes, it makes more sense to have a pedal on the opposite side of the board from the pedals that it will need to be plugged into, so you may need to plan for some custom cable lengths in between each pedal. For example, you may want a wah pedal to be on the left side of your board, near the output, but it should go first in the chain, so you'll have to run the cables to the opposite side of the board where the next pedal in the chain is physically located.

However you decide to design your board, you should have it setup so that there is as little wear and tear on cables as possible. There's nothing worse than getting to a show and having to try and track down a bad cable on your pedalboard before you can soundcheck.

Pedals vs. Processors

Personally, I prefer the sound of pedals and amps to processors, but processors *are* very appealing to a lot of guitarists because they are durable, relatively easy to program, and easy to setup and tear down. If you decide to go with a processor setup, I would recommend an amp-modeling software system, like the Line 6 POD or something similar. With amp-modeling the effects in the processor will sound much better than processors without amp-modeling.

Tip #44: Pickups

The pickups are the heart of an electric guitar. Depending on their construction and position on the body, they can have a wide variety of tones from thin, clear, and glassy, to thick, dark, and creamy. Every pickup model will have a unique tone and will work with the wood on your guitar in a different way. In general, though, there are a few common types of pickups with shared traits that we will discuss here.

Single-Coil Pickups

Single-coils are usually found on Fender-style guitars. They are made with six magnets, called pole pieces (one for each string), which are wound by hair-thin copper wire. The vibration of the strings activates an electrical field within the copper and magnets of the pickup, which then translates into an audio signal for your amp. Single-coils are typically glassy and clear sounding, with decreased midrange and increased highs and lows. They are used a lot in country, classic rock, and blues music, but aren't suited for many high-gain applications because they tend to be fairly noisy.

Humbucking Pickups

Humbuckers are made by taking two single-coils and placing them next to each other with the direction of the copper windings going opposite directions. The effect of this is, as the name suggests, is that the "hum" or noise is canceled out by the opposing direction of the coils. Humbuckers are common on just about every type of guitar, including many Fender models because of their thick, creamy, mid-range heavy tone and their ability to be used with high gain pedals and amps without making an ungodly amount of noise. They are often used in rock, metal, blues, and jazz applications.

P-90s

Somewhere in between a single-coil and a humbucker is the P-90. Originally developed by Gibson, this classic pickup – sometimes referred to as a "soap bar" - is technically a large, overwound single-coil. The effect of this is that it retains some of the single-coil characteristics, such as clarity and brightness, with the thick mid-range and creamy quality of a humbucker. The major drawback of P-90s is that they are noisy – even more so than standard single-coils. There are ways around this, though, as we'll see in an upcoming section.

Pickup Position

Besides the type, the tone of a pickup will also be influenced by its position on the guitar body. Typically, one pickup will be placed close to the neck (called the neck pickup), and one will be placed close to the bridge (called the bridge pickup), and in many single coil models there will be a third pickup in the middle (called the middle pickup).

Bridge pickups will tend to have a brighter tone than the others. This is because the string vibrates at shorter distances closer to the bridge, so the high frequencies are more pronounced.

Neck pickups are thicker and warmer than the bridge pickup because the strings are vibrating at longer distances toward the middle, and the lower frequencies are more pronounced.

Most guitars – even if they only have two pickups – will have a middle position that allows you to access two pickups at once. This creates a tone that is more balanced between highs and lows.

Buffers and Shielding

One drawback of passive single-coil pickups is that they produce a relatively weak signal. If you are using a lot of pedals with passive single-coils, you may want to consider using pedals that have built in buffers – circuits which help boost the signal throughout the pedal chain – or a standalone buffer pedal. This will ensure that the signal stays strong throughout its journey from guitar to amp. The other drawback, that I mentioned earlier, is noise. Noise can be reduced greatly by shielding your guitar. On a Strat-style guitar, you can line the underside of the pick-guard with copper foil (available at most hardware stores – even self-adhesive varieties), and that will help a lot with the noise. For P-90s, there often isn't a pickguard to use, so you'll have to actually line the pickup cavities themselves with copper foil.

Power

Tip #45: How to Power Your Gear

There are a lot of different ways to get electricity flowing through your signal chain. Not all of them are equal, however. Most amplifiers these days use a standard C13 connector cable (the kind used for most computers) and are well grounded. Vintage amplifiers, however, may have older wiring setups that aren't grounded well. These should **definitely** be plugged into a power conditioner to avoid safety hazards and excessive noise.

As for pedals, if you're only using one or two, you can probably get away with using separate power supplies for each one, though you may have to bring a couple of power strips with you. One alternative for a handful of pedals is to use a power-supply daisy-chain setup. There are a lot of varieties and brands to choose from, but the basic principle is that you have one "wall wart," or adapter, that runs five or six pedals through a daisy chain of connectors. This is a decent option if you're running mostly quiet effects like modulation or delay. High gain effects like distortion, fuzz, or compression may be too noisy with this method, though.

The best option for powering multiple pedals is to use some sort of power conditioner, such as a Voodoo Lab Pedal Power 2 Plus, or a similar brand. These units will send an isolated power signal to each individual pedal, keeping it from interfering with, or being interfered with by the other pedals in the chain. Many of these units also have variable voltage levels to simulate dying batteries on vintage effects, which can create some really cool tones.

Choosing the Right Power Supply

Most pedals will give you the power requirements somewhere on the underside of the unit or in the user manual. Typically stomp boxes run on a 9VDC circuit at 300mA with a reversed polarity plug. The Boss PSA power supply will run most stomp-boxes, but some vintage or unique models will have different

power requirements and will need a specialized
adapter.

Power Conditioners

A surge-protecting power strip or two are required
items for your accessory bag. You can use these to
plug in all of your gear, and they will help somewhat
with noise and grounding issues. You don't
necessarily need the fanciest one, but some form of
surge protection is a must.

Tip #46: Stands, Straps, and Strings

Stands

Stands can be a real pain when it comes to saving
space on the tour. The cheap ones are awkwardly
shaped, as are some of the more expensive models. I
recommend either a multi-guitar rack (on which the
entire band can store their guitars), or a couple of the
compact A-frame designs that are available. If you
can't bring either of these designs with you, you will
want to think about possibly storing all stands in a
box or bin. This will save you a lot of space and
headache when it comes time to load the van or
trailer.

Straps

Make sure you get a comfortable strap - especially if you're going to be playing long sets. You probably won't notice it as much with a Strat or other light-bodied guitar, but Les Pauls and the like can get very heavy after a couple of hours. A wide leather strap, or one that has some padding will help your back and the rest of your body in the long one. Also, as mentioned above, make sure you put some kind of strap-lock system on your guitar in order to avert disaster.

Strings

Most guitarists use nickel strings for electric guitars and bronze strings for acoustics. Nickel strings have a well-balanced tone and are fairly resilient. Some string brands also manufacture stainless steel strings for electrics. These are brighter sounding and a little stronger.

Choose a gage that is comfortable for you. I typically use .010 - .046 (regular) gage strings for my electrics and .012 - .053 for acoustics. Lighter gage strings are easier to bend and play over all, but their tone is thinner and not as strong. Heavier gage strings have a thick, rich tone, but bending them can prove difficult.

As for brand, I honestly haven't found a big difference in sound or durability between the different brands out there. There is a lot of chatter on the internet over how many factories actually manufacture strings and whether or not many string "brands" are actually just re-packaged generic strings, but the majority of the big names do make their own strings. The key is to find a gage and a material that works for you. The brand is secondary.

Tip #47: Tuners

I highly recommend putting a tuner-pedal on your pedalboard. Stand-alone tuners may be cheaper, or in some cases more expensive and technically more accurate (strobe tuners, etc.), but for practical application, you just can't beat a Boss-style tuner on your board. Make sure that the display is bright enough to see while you're on stage, and that the tuner has a mute function, so that the audience doesn't have to listen to you tune up between songs.

If you're bringing a guitar tech with you, you will probably want two tuners. Ideally, the tech should have a stand-alone unit backstage to tune the guitars you're not using.

Chapter 4: Life on the Road

Whether you're going on tour for a week or a month, traveling with your band can present some unique challenges that aren't always present when you're traveling for fun. Road delays, fatigue, and weather issues can all turn a simple trip from city to city into an odyssey in a heartbeat, so it's best to be prepared and to keep your attitude as flexible as possible. From safe driving tips to dealing with boredom, this chapter will give you some tips for making sure your trip goes smoothly.

Safe Driving Tips

The first and most important thing to remember is that you can't play a great show if you're dead, in the hospital, or in jail – all of which are potential consequences of unsafe driving. In addition to yourself, you have a responsibility to your bandmates and the other drivers on the road to ensure that both your vehicle and your driving are safe.

Tip #48: Inspect Your Vehicle

Before you head out, you should take some time to make sure that your vehicle is in safe working order. It's best to do this a day or two before you leave, so that if you need to replace anything or make arrangements for a different vehicle, you have time to do it. If you're not mechanically inclined, it may be worth it to take your vehicle to a trusted mechanic for an inspection. If you'd rather do it yourself, here are some things you should definitely check before you leave:

- Antifreeze/Coolant
- Belts (should be tight, not worn or frayed)
- Engine oil
- Transmission/differential oil
- Hoses (check for leaks and make sure all fittings are tight)
- Brakes
- Battery
- Signals, lights, and indicators
- Tire pressure

Once you've checked all of these things, you may want to do a test drive to listen for noises or see if there are any other issues before you head out for real.

Tip #49: Make a Driving Schedule

For any legs of the trip during which you will be doing more than four or five hours of driving, you should work out a driver schedule. Make sure that whomever is behind the wheel is licensed, insured, alert, and responsible. I don't recommend driving more than ten hours in a day, especially if you need to play that night. Try to schedule your tour so that you can get to the next city in a few hours of driving.

Tip #50: Pack Well

Part of your safety considerations should be how your gear is packed. Try not to obstruct your view out the rear window, and be sure that your mirrors are adjusted and functional. Loose items piled up in the back of hatchbacks or vans may fly forward during sudden stops, so make sure you tie everything down – even if it's inside the van.

Equipment in trailers should be balanced so that the weight is evenly distributed to avoid undue strain on the hitch. Too much weight at the rear of the trailer can cause the hitch to raise slightly, resulting in less traction on the rear wheels. Too much weight at the front of the trailer can cause the hitch to sink, potentially leading to road damage.

Similarly, make sure the cab of the vehicle is clear of unnecessary clutter which may hinder the driver's ability to operate the vehicle safely. The driver should have unrestricted access to all vehicle controls and should have a clear view out of all windows and mirrors.

Tip #51: Winter Driving

If you're from the southern latitudes, you may not have much experience driving in snowy or icy conditions. Traveling through severe weather can be nerve-wracking at best, and deadly at worst.

The most important thing to remember about winter driving is to **slow down.** You *have* to drive slowly in the snow and ice. If the speed limit is 60 miles per hour and it's snowing or icy, you should drive much more slowly. Speed limits assume ideal conditions, and snow and ice are anything but ideal. Even if you have all-wheel drive, that only helps you go – it doesn't help you stop. Stopping distances are much farther on ice and snow.

Remember that other drivers are probably having just as much trouble with the weather as you are, and they may not be able to stop or go as you would expect them to. Your senses need to be sharp and you need to drive as defensively as possible.

Pack enough emergency equipment, and make sure that it's seasonally appropriate. In addition to a first aid kit, flares, jumper cables, and other safety gear, you will also want to bring a blanket or two, some extra clothing, and some candles in case you get stranded.

Tip #52: Things to Avoid

- Do not, under any circumstances, drive under the influence of alcohol, drugs, or prescription medication which can impair motor functions. Your life and the lives of other innocent people are at stake.
- Do not drive when you're too tired. This is as bad or worse than driving under the influence.

- Do not check text messages, e-mails, or use your phone while driving. Have a passenger do these things.
- Do not drive if weather conditions are prohibitive and you can avoid it.

Tip #53: Gas Stations

Refueling stops are a huge part of life on the road, and while most gas stations will have the basics, there *are* good and bad choices. Aside from checking for the lowest gas prices (which is definitely important), you may need some other supplies that many smaller gas stations may not have.

Best Options

If you're low on fuel, you probably can't be picky when it comes to picking a gas station – any port in a storm, and all that. So if the needle is teasing empty and there's a gas station coming up, use it. If you have a couple of choices, however, these are some things you want in a gas station:

- Large stores with new displays and signs. These will most likely have a good selection of drinks, snacks, and accessories.
- Air and water stations.
- Fast food restaurants.
- Lots of pumps.

From public restrooms to basic automotive supplies, many locally-owned small town gas stations will simply not have what you need. In order to make the most out of each stop, try to go to larger gas stations with bigger stores. If you can, use truck stops.

Truck Stops and Travel Plazas

Most major interstate highways will have one or two of these outside of each significant town or city you pass. They are heaven. They usually have showers and convenience stores that could rival some small-town strip malls. In a truck stop, you'll often be able to buy everything from a new set of clothes to a tablet or a laptop. There are usually one or two fast food restaurants, as well as the typical selection of convenience store junk food.

Convenience Food

It is very easy to eat terribly when you're on the road. It's also not too difficult to eat healthy, if you know what to look for. Almost every gas station or truck stop you come to will have a similar selection of preservative-laden, fat-filled hot dogs, taquitos, corn dogs, chicken strips, and fries. They will also usually have a smorgasbord of chips, candy bars, and cookies. If you're only touring for a weekend, this kind of salty, sugary indulgence can seem all too appealing, but if you're out for a month or more, eating those types of foods can really throw your health and energy for a loop.

Many of the larger gas stations and truck stops will have some kind of fast food restaurant inside. Most of these restaurants have healthy options available. Beyond that, the convenience store may have cold sandwiches or pre-made salads that are relatively healthy.

If you can't find any salds or sandwiches, try to avoid chips and sweets. Beef jerky is salty, but other than that it's high in protein and low in fat, which will help keep your energy up.

Credit Cards and Rewards Programs

In addition to store credit cards, a lot of the larger gas-station chains will have rewards or loyalty card programs. These programs can save you quite a bit of money if used properly. They often feature fuel and snack discounts based on the number of points you earn by spending money with them. These discounts – especially on fuel – can really add up when you're putting in a few thousand miles. Similarly, some credit cards (either oil company cards or other major credit cards) will also have rewards or cash-back programs for fuel, so make sure you're taking advantage of all of the savings and discounts available to you.

Fun Times

Let's not forget that touring should be fun, too! There are all kinds of great jokes, pranks, and games to play, but make sure that you're not taking things too far.

Tip #54: Joking Around on the Road

Of course, everyone's sense of humor is different, and every band is going to have its own inside jokes. From trying to convince your bandmates that your early childhood was actually the plot of _The Wizard_ - the relatively obscure '90s movie starring Fred Savage - to more classic dorm-style pranks like drawing on sleeping faces with a magic marker, there are as many ways to get one over on each other as there are people in the world.

My only caution here is to know when it's appropriate to joke and when it's probably best to wait. If you're in a relatively new band and you haven't spent a lot of time together, you may not know what's likely to upset or offend one of your bandmates, and excess tension is not something anyone needs on the road. What may be hilarious to you may be deeply painful for someone else, so try to be aware of that if you don't know your bandmates as well as you know your family yet. The good news is, after a week or two of traveling together, you'll know those bandmates really well, and you'll share a bond that not many other people get to share.

Making the Most of the Miles

On one of our trips, our bass player introduced us to
Cards Against Humanity. At the time, the now wildly
popular card game was in its infancy and they were
offering free .pdf versions of the original card packs
online to download. The bass player downloaded
these files and spent a couple of hours copying them
onto index cards while we were driving. Once he was
done, we played for the rest of that leg of the trip,
which was a ridiculous number of hours. When we
got home, we all agreed that his actions that day saved
our sanity.

A deck of cards, or other types of games that are easily
played in the car can be a godsend. When you're
driving through Eastern Wyoming, and the only
things you've seen for 200 miles are cattle and
scrublands, a game of five card draw, rummy, or even
Go Fish can be refreshing.

Another thing that can help keep things interesting is
to play games with the music you pick. Taking turns
picking songs and making them subject to ridiculous
rules can actually be quite fun – especially with a car
full of musicians.

Make sure to also schedule time during your drives to
stop for any historical or interesting roadside
attractions. For example, in Southeastern
Washingon, there's a monument that was inspired by
Stonehenge and looks similar. Also, if you're passing
through cities or towns with unique attractions you
should definitely take time to go and see them. From
the troll underneath the Freemont bridge in Seattle

and Oldtown in San Diego to the Riverwalk in San Antonio and Beale Street in Memphis, each part of the country has something unique to offer. It would be a shame to miss out on any of it.

Tip #55: Neck Issues (People)

When you're packing the car, remember that you're all going to be spending a lot of time in there. Of course, all of your gear and other baggage needs to fit, but you also have to have room to stretch a little. Cramps and other musculoskeletal issues can cause real problems in both the short term and the long term. Aside from just being a literal pain in the neck, stiff muscles and joints can zap your energy. A lack of energy combined with soreness and stiffness will definitely affect your performance.

The easiest way to avoid this is to pack so that you have room to change positions in your seat from time to time. Try not to put too many people in the vehicle, either. Just because a car or van _says_ it can fit seven people, doesn't mean it can fit seven people **and** whole band's worth of luggage and gear.

Maintaining a generally good fitness level will help you in more ways than one can count when it comes to performance and stamina. An active lifestyle filled with regular exercise will allow your body to store the energy it needs and release it efficiently when you're on stage each night. One way to keep yourself limber and full of energy is to incorporate a short five-minute stretching routine into each rest stop. Make sure to stretch all of your limbs, your back, and your neck. If you're not already using a stretching or exercise routine, talk to a doctor or healthcare professional before starting one.

Tip #56: Tacos (After-Show Care)

One of the band traditions we've come to love in my band is post-show tacos. Wherever we are, we try to find a good taco truck or Mexican restaurant that's open late so that we can get tacos and wind down after the show. It's a simple thing, but it can really help the general morale of a long tour and it can help bring you and your bandmates closer together. Of course, it doesn't have to be tacos. Be it gas-station hot dogs, or any number of other potential pre or post-show rituals, ensuring that you care for yourself and each other goes a long way to ensuring a successful tour

Chapter 5: Putting On a Great Show

Acoustics

Ever notice how a bouncing basketball sounds very different on concrete than when it's dribbled on a gymnasium floor? Even though the source of the sound – an inflated basketball being driven against a hard surface – is the same, the actual sounds we hear are very different. This difference is explained by acoustics. "Acoustics" refers to the science of sound wave propagation. It explains how sound waves interact with their physical environment, and how that environment shapes the way the sound waves behave.

Every room – whether it's a large dance hall or a small club – has its own unique acoustic properties. These properties are influenced by the volume (amount of cubic space) of the room, the materials used in building the room, and the number of people in the room, just to name a few. Because of these acoustic differences, you may find you need to make some adjustments to your gear in order to get the best tone you can get for the show.

Tip #57: General Principles

If you're in a large room like a gym or a ballroom, you will most likely have to deal with a lot of natural reverb. As I mentioned before, this reverb can really play havoc on your tone – especially if you add more reverb to your tone with an effects processor or stomp box. For the most part, you want to limit the amount of reverb you use in such rooms. Delay will probably be okay, but you may even want to turn that down a bit.

Hardwood floors, walls, and ceilings wall also give you a lot of natural reverb, as will an empty room. On the other hand, if you have carpeted floors, soft materials on the walls, and acoustic paneling on the ceiling, you won't have nearly as much natural reverb, so the tone will be easier to manage.

Tune the Room

If you do find yourself in a less-than-ideal acoustic environment, you will probably need to make some adjustments. Don't be afraid to tweak your EQ settings or your drive/gain levels. Try to work with the sound technician to see if you can get the sweet-spot dialed in. You may also have to lower your stage volume so that the tech can fine tune the sound more accurately during soundcheck.

Tip #58: Basic Audio Principles

It's the sound technician's job to make sure the PA system is working well, and that the overall sound is clear and well-balanced. Unfortunately, the supply of well-qualified sound technicians is often meager. I've played shows where the sound techs have absolutely no idea what they're doing all to often. Once when I was opening for a nationally touring act, the club's sound tech showed up nearly two hours late and was obviously high. Despite these situations, the old adage still holds true – the show must go on. Therefore, a basic understanding of how to mix a band is a good thing to have.

Most sound boards will have multiple channels with separate controls in addition to the master control section. The individual channels will each have, at the minimum, a gain control, a level control, a pan control, and some kind of EQ controls. The gain knob controls the input level – or how sensitive the microphone is - while the level controls the output – or how loud the microphone is.

If you're experiencing feedback or squealing, try adjusting the gain first. This will often take care of the problem. If that doesn't work, try adjusting the EQ.

EQ controls will usually consist of knobs for high frequencies, low frequencies, and mid-range frequencies. Some boards will also allow you to set the center frequency of the mid control. High frequencies usually range from 4kHz to 12kHz and are sometimes referred to as *treble*. If the high frequency control is set too high, squealing feedback can result and the sound can actually be painful. Low frequencies usually range from 80Hz to 400Hz and are referred to collectively as *bass*. Too much bass in the mix can result in very loud and persistent rumbling feedback. Similarly, the mid-range frequencies cover the range between 400Hz and

4kHz. If the center frequency of this control is set too high or low, feedback can also result.

When attempting to solve noise or feedback problems, make changes in small increments so that you're changing the overall sound too drastically.

Levels

While it's true that some amps – especially vintage tube amps – have a "sweet spot" in their volume range, it doesn't necessarily follow that the amp should always be set to that volume level. In large arenas or outdoor venues, stage volume may not be very important, as there is a lot more room for the sound to dissipate, but in smaller clubs, too much volume can kill the sound. Make sure that you're not overpowering your audience.

Microphone Placement

The placement of the microphone can also affect its tone. If you're having a hard time dialing in the tone you want, try changing where you place the mic. Sometimes it may be best to place the microphone right up against the grill cloth in the center of the speaker at a perpendicular angle. Other times, placing the mic toward the outer edge of the speaker, back from the grill a couple of inches, and at an axis will be much better. The key is to find the best placement for each room.

Acoustic guitars are usually best mic'd right in front of the sound hole, but sometimes it might be best to move the mic more toward either the body or the neck of the guitar to balance out the tone.

Tip #59: Mix

This may be hard to believe, but unless you're a solo act, you're not the only one on stage. It's only human for us to pay attention to our own sound more than we're paying attention to the rest of the band, but you need to keep in mind that the audience needs to hear the whole band, not just you. This is why we have stage monitors.

Sometimes, however, a bad mix has less to do with our egos and more to do with the tone coming from our amplifiers. Some musical styles – I'm thinking of heavy metal specifically – demand guitar tones that are just not conducive to a good mix. The problem is that a lot of times the mid-range is "scooped out," or turned all the way down. The problem is that most notes played on the guitar fall within those midrange frequencies, so if you turn those frequencies down, you're, in effect, turning the guitar down. By itself, an amplifier with the midrange turned up might sound less-than-desirable, but in a mix with the rest of the band, it will cut through and sing like nobody's business.

If you want to boost your tone just for leads, an EQ pedal might work well. Models like the Boss GE-7 will allow you to boost or cut specific frequencies, and they also have a gain control, so you can increase the overall volume for leads as well.

Also, as mentioned before, too much reverb can also bury your guitar in the mix. Don't use reverb in a live setting unless it's an important part of the song. Just don't.

Tip #60: Monitors

Monitors are there so that you can hear your guitar and your voice above the rest of the band and make sure that you're playing the right notes. Some venues have great monitor systems that allow for each member of the band to get his or her own mix, while others may not have any monitors at all. Knowing what you need in the monitors can make a big difference in the quality of the show – after all, if you can't hear yourself, you may not even know if you're making mistakes.

Most venues will have a monitor system consisting of a single wedge-shaped speaker placed on the stage in front of each performer. Sometimes, though, these speakers may be daisy-chained together, which means that all of them will have the same mix. In those cases, the whole band will need to agree on what the monitor mix sounds like. Individual preferences will vary, but if you have the luxury of choosing your mix, make sure you're as specific as possible so that you can put on a great show.

Some players prefer in-ear monitor systems. These systems are usually cost prohibitive for the venue to own, but most modern sound systems will be compatible with them if you want to bring your own with you. I personally prefer open-air speakers (I like to hear more of what the audience is hearing – headphones make me feel too isolated), but many people like the isolated mix that in-ear systems provide.

Tip #61: Quiet! Avoiding Noise

Whenever you've got a bunch of high-powered audio equipment all running on the same circuit, noise is bound to happen. Usually, it shows up in the form of what's commonly referred to as "sixty-cycle hum." This is a low, persistent hum at 60Hz that happens when there are grounding issues or other electrical interference. To avoid this, use surge protectors and try to use multiple electrical circuits when plugging in gear. Ground-lifts on direct-boxes or bass amplifiers can also help to reduce this problem. If you have a large pedalboard with a lot of individual pedals, you may want to consider a noise gate.

RF Interference

If you opt for a wireless system instead of cables, you may encounter problems with radio frequency (RF) interference. This happens when the wireless system is transmitting and receiving on frequencies that are too close to other frequencies in use by radio stations or other communication devices. Using multiple wireless systems operating on close frequencies can also cause problems. If you're going to buy a wireless system, make sure to get one that has variable frequencies, so that you can change them if you need to.

Unplugging

It might seem like a small thing, but it'll peg you as a rookie faster than just about anything else. When the show is over, or if you need to switch guitars in between songs, DO NOT JUST UNPLUG YOUR GUITAR. If you have a tuner on your pedalboard, it probably has a mute function. If you have a volume pedal, you can use it to mute your signal before unplugging. If you don't have either of these, then you can either turn your amp off or switch it to "Standby" before unplugging. Failure to take any of these precautions will cause what we call "the bad noise" - a very loud pop that can damage both speakers and eardrums.

Tip #62: The Audience

If a band plays a show in a forest, and there's nobody there to hear them, did they make a sound? Of course they do, but who cares? The audience is the most important part of the show. Period. All of the practice, professionalism, and preparation in the world don't add up to anything if there aren't any butts in the seats. Making sure that the audience has a good time is priority number one, though sometimes that's easier said than done.

Who is your audience?

Just like a business needs to understand its customer base (or *market*), successful bands should have a good grasp on what type of people like their music and will pay to come see their shows. However, knowing the audience you'd like to have and being able to read the audience that's in front of you are often two different things.

Just as each band will have its own unique collection of fans, a club or venue may also have a reputation for attracting a certain type of clientele. Typically club owners and promoters will try to match up bands when creating a bill for a show, but it's not uncommon for them to just add any available band if one of the original acts backs out, or if they just need the spot filled. In these cases, it's entirely possible to have a blues roots band opening up for a hardcore rap-metal band. If the rap-metal band has a big following, the crowd might be made up entirely of their fans – fans who may not appreciate the subtleties of your style. In these cases, set lists may need to be adjusted to suit the situation. Try to pick songs that the audience members will respond to.

Also, make sure you keep your audience in mind when addressing the crowd between songs. If you're

playing in an outdoor space like a park, you may want
to refrain from using profanity or doing anything that
may be offensive to families or children (unless, of
course, you're *trying* to shock people – a la Alice
Cooper, Ozzy, Kiss, or Marilyn Manson).

Dealing with Drunks and Hecklers

No matter what type of performing you do, eventually
you will come across some jerk in the audience who
has either had too much to drink, or who can't stand
the idea of someone else taking all of the room's
attention. These people should be dealt with
immediately. Remember that if they're annoying you
they're probably annoying the rest of the audience,
too.

Typically, a few well-placed smart-ass remarks will
put the offender in his or her place, but occasionally
more drastic measures are needed. Remember,
though, that *you're* the professional. You have more
to lose than the drunk or heckler does. Do not get into
a physical altercation unless you absolutely need to
defend yourself or someone else. I've had to stop
songs occasionally to call out someone who's behavior
is bothering other audience members, but this should
be a last resort. If you need to have someone removed
from the club, talk to security or another staff
member.

Tip #63: How to Connect with Your Audience

One of the first concerts I attended when I was young was the G3 tour with Steve Vai, Joe Satriani, and Eric Johnson. I was really excited to see the three guitar virtuosos, especially Eric Johnson, who was my favorite at the time. When I saw them all in concert, though, my opinion changed. Instead, Joe Satriani, whom I was least excited to see, became my favorite.

It wasn't that Satriani played better songs, or that his playing was more technical, or even that his tone was better. It was the show he put on. You see, Eric Johnson played the second set of the show, and I don't think he addressed the audience or even really looked at us at all during that set. He just stood in one spot, looked down at his guitar, and played with gigantic studio headphones on. It looked like he was just in his own little world and it didn't matter if I was there or not. If I had just closed my eyes and put on headphones, Johnson would have still taken the cake, but I can do that in the comfort of my own home. If I'm going to shell out the money and make the effort to go to a show, the band had better give me some extra value.

The point here is that it's not enough to just play the songs perfectly. Audiences expect some kind of an experience beyond that. There are a lot of ways to make a show interesting, from adding theatrics and stagecraft elements to great banter between band and audience members. If nobody in your band has an especially extroverted personality, then you might want to think about adding special lights or some other kind of visual stimulation to your show. On the other hand, if you've got a real spaz in the band that loves the spotlight, let him or her have free reign to connect with the audience.

Telling jokes or funny stories can endear a band to its audience, as can silly banter between songs. Audience participation is also a great way to build rapport, but it works best if the audience knows the song. In other words, asking the audience to sing along with one of your songs that they're just hearing for the first time is a whole different animal than asking the audience to sing along with the chorus of "Sweet Caroline."

Someone from the band should always be available after the show to talk to fans, too. Personally, this is my least favorite part of the show, as I am not very good at small talk or connecting with people I don't know well. On the other hand, I understand the importance of this part of the job, and I will gladly spend some time at the merch booth after the show if there are people there.

Performance

From dealing with nerves to writing the set list, there are myriad elements that go into making a great show. As with so many other things, a hundred things can go right during a performance, but all it takes is one thing to go wrong for it to all come crashing down. This section will offer some tips and advice on how to tie up as many loose ends as possible before showtime.

Tip #64: Nerves

During one of my very first public performances when I was in high school, I was set to sing the Eagles' "Desperado," in front of about a hundred and fifty people or so. I started the song exactly like I'd rehearsed, except I was so focused on making sure I played the introduction correctly that I didn't realize I'd started singing the third verse in place of the first until it was too late. Ordinarily, this wouldn't be a very big deal – one can usually substitute one verse for another without too much of a problem – but with that song, the third verse leads into a coda that resolves and ends the song, and there's no easy way to recover from it. I ended up having to stop the song mid-verse and start again.

Stage fright can wreak havoc on a person. A little bit of anxiety can be a good thing, but too much can cause paralysis or a complete blank-out. Luckily for me, it's usually not an issue. This is not to say that I don't still get a little nervous every time I step onstage in front of a large crowd, but over the years I've learned to channel that anxiety into energy for the performance.

Nearly every musician I know has some sort of pre-show routine or ritual that helps to steady and center them. For me, I like to hang out in the green room and play guitar or chat with other musicians. Some people like to put headphones on and bury themselves in a game on their phone. They usually say that it's their way of blocking out the world and getting in the right headspace.

No matter what your ritual looks like, you want to try to turn that anxious energy into performance energy. One other bit of caution, though, when converting this energy, is to make sure you don't rush your set too much. High adrenaline and cortisol levels resulting from pre-show excitement can send tempos rocketing into the stratosphere. An onstage light-display metronome may be a good investment if this is a consistent issue.

Tip #65: Writing a Set List

Just like there's an art to creating the perfect playlist for a party, there's an art to creating a great setlist, too.

In addition to considering time, you'll also want to consider your audience, other bands that are on the bill, and the overall flow of the energy level. Let's look at a couple of scenarios and see what the process for writing the setlist may look like.

Scenario 1: You are an opening act and you have a 40-minute set. Your music is acoustic roots rock, but the band you're opening for is more of a heavy blues band. For a set like this, you'll want to start out with some energy. Pick your most popular up-tempo number and start with that. Assuming each song averages around five minutes, you have time for seven or eight songs, so the next one should be up-tempo as well. Then you can mellow things out a bit with a slower song or two. By the fifth song, though, the energy level had better be way back up, so you may even want to throw a popular cover in at that point to keep the crowd with you. That energy level should stay up for last couple of songs, and you should end with a spectacle. If you've got any songs that call for crowd participation, or epic guitar solos, this is the time to play them.

Scenario 2: You are headlining a small festival with a large crowd of all ages. In this scenario, you may want to skip any offensive songs because of the family environment. As a headliner, you have a lot more freedom to be creative with your set. I've had success doing long, drawn-out introductions with instrumental mp3s playing in the background, a stage covered with fog, and each band member coming on at the same time. I've also had success coming out and starting the set off with a capella vocals. In either of these scenarios, however, you want your set list to have a a sort of energy arc, where it ebbs and flows a bit to keep people interested.

Tip #66: Stage Plots and Blocking

Many promoters will ask for a stage plot in the contract for the gig or during your conversations about logistics. A stage plot is simply a diagram of where you and your gear will be on stage. I've written out stage plots on napkins, and I've used hi-tech apps to build them. The promoter, stage manager, or venue owner may have his or her own formatting requirements, but if you use an app (I use one called Napkin Sketch – _ironic, I know_), most promoters and the like won't scoff. As long as you can export your stage plot to a .jpg or .pdf file, it should be fine.

A good stage plot will have a scale layout of the stage, the position of each performer, the position of each amplifier, drum/percussion set, keyboard, monitor, microphone stand, and any other extraneous equipment that is important to the show. Iron Maiden, famous for their legendary theatrical shows with giant zombie puppets and pyrotechnics, comes to mind. All of those things need to be carefully mapped out on a stage plot.

Tip #67: Blocking

There's a legendary story from the '90s in which Metallica frontman and rhythm guitarist James Hetfield was too close to a pyrotechnic devise and was severely burned as a result. Hetfield had to cancel the rest of the show (obviously), and had to continue the multi-million dollar tour with a hired rhythm guitarist while his arm healed. Your stage plot may not have anything that dangerous, but it's still a good idea for all parties involved to know the stage plot and the location of their marks before the show starts.

Some bands also make dynamic movement and choreography a part of thier shows. If you are in one such band or desire to be, then you'll need to do a lot of blocking rehearsal. It should also probably go without saying that if you have band members moving around a lot on stage, with theatrics and all, then you should be using wireless systems instead of cables for your guitars. See the section on these on page 59 for further information about coordinating frequencies. Switching sides of the stage at key intervals, guitarists climbing drum risers and harassing them, singers appearing from the wings after long instrumental sections – all of these things need to be rehearsed and blocked out for maximum effect.

Tip #68: Basic Stagecraft

The first time a frontman ever climbed a lighting rig and did a stage dive, it was pure rock and roll glory. Then everyone started to do it, and it became a cliché. Similarly, gratuitous or randomly added prop effects like giant puppets, pyrotechnics, lasers, and the like have also become rock and roll tropes of sorts. If you're playing in a low-budget touring blues/rock, country, jazz, or really any non-metal band, you can probably ignore this section. On the other hand, if you play seven-string guitars tuned three steps down and your lead vocalist sounds like the Cookie Monster, pay attention.

- **What effect are you really trying to create?** Are you trying to create a brooding, goth rock atmosphere? Then darkness and makeup, though easily turned into tropes, can also be an asset if it's done tastefully. Remember that some of the best horror movies never show you the monster.
- **Taste**. Unless you want to be the next GWAR, refrain from insulting, offending, or covering your audience with gooey substances.

- **Choreography.** Steel Panther gets away with tight spandex, four cans of hairspray and running across the stage with cucumbers in their trousers because they've fully committed to the schtick. Unless you're an '80s tribute band, try not to stand next to your other guitar player and sway back and forth with the tempo of the power ballad you're currently churning out.
- **Be nice to the light tech.** If he/she likes you, they will go out of their way to pick up on musical cues and make your show so much better than it would be if they just sat behind the board and changed colors every so often.
- **Costumes/Wardrobe.** I've played shows in formal dress attire, and I've played in a Hawaiian shirt, board shorts, and Crocs. Sometimes the occasion calls for some flashy clothes. Sometimes it doesn't. The point is, put some thought into how you'd like to look for each show. As a general rule, a nice set of jeans will do, as will a couple of well-fitting button-down or pearl-snap shirts.

I have a few very nice stage shirts that I purchased from a western clothing store, and I usually end up wearing them for larger venue shows, while for club shows a t-shirt and jeans is usually appropriate for my band/audience.

Random costume pieces can be a lot of fun, as well. Ridiculous hats are my favorite.

Tip #69: On-Stage Behavior

You're up there to be entertaining, so for God's sake, entertain. Remember the anecdote about Eric Johnson I shared earlier. His playing was flawless, but I could have saved my money and had just as interesting an experience had I stayed home and listened to the album. Having a good rapport with your bandmates, as well as with your audience is crucial.

Look at your bandmates and smile at them. Even if you've been on the road for two months and the bass player's snoring is making you want to punch puppies, on stage, he or she needs to look like your best friend to the audience. You really think Mick Jagger and Keith Richards want to spend any more time in a room together after all these years than is absolutely necessary to maintain the Stones' empire? Yet, when you see them on stage, Keith smiles at Mick, and Mick puts his arm around his ol' pal Keef.

Between songs, do not talk over one another. If several people in the band have microphones, you need to be conscientious that you're not speaking over or on top of each other while introducing songs or thanking the audience. If you find this happening a lot, I suggest you actually work out a script (formally written down or not) for your onstage banter. I've did it for years with my drummer and bass player when I was the front-man for a cover band.

Of course, the most important people for you to connect with are the audience members. At the very least look them in the eye. Maynard Keenan (Tool) gets away with standing with his back toward the audience because his fans know the legend of his agoraphobia. Your fans likely do not know nearly that much about you and will not take kindly to being ignored. Throw a pick or two out after each song. Bend down and talk to the people in the front row – they love that! Keep coming back to certain individuals and connect with a nod or a smile, or even just point your guitar at them during a solo. Every audience member wants to feel special, and you're the center of attention in that moment, so you have the power to make that person feel great.

Tip #70: Beginnings and Endings

Like so much else we've discussed here, there's a difference between creating a great song for an album in the studio and creating a great performance of a song. If you have a very artsty-type song with a long intro and a lot of samples or other ear-candy on the record, how are you going to recreate that live? Do you really need to recreate it live, or can you come up with another intro for the song that's as interesting as the one on the record. For example, one of my songs, California Sky, appears on an EP we recorded that has a concept running through the whole album. There are radio signals and recurring musical passages in between each song, and California Sky in particular just starts with two drum hits and a walk down from G to Em. It'd be pretty complicated to carry around a flash drive with the audio from the record and have the sound guy remember to play it before the song during our set. Instead, we just worked out an intro where we sing the chorus a cappella and then go into the big two-hit intro.

Endings provide similar challenges. For whatever reason, so many song fade out on the recordings. Without a lot of practice and careful choreography, you can't really pull this off easily in a live environment. It *can* be done, but you've gotta be committed and have a lot of volume pedals on stage. Instead, most bands opt for coming up with a special ending for the live version.

The easiest and most common way to do this is to pick the last chord of the song, hold it out with a lot of crashing cymbals and tremolo strumming and other nonsense for a minute or so. This is commonly referred to as the crash-bang ending.

Another way similar to the crash-bang ending is to simply play the final note of the chorus or outro of the song staccato. Or you could just let the last chord ring out without all of the drum crashing, etc. Sometimes, it's even fun to add new riffs and sections to the end of a song, too.

Tip #71: Opening the Show

Whether you're the only band on the bill, opening for other local acts, or opening for a big national act, the responsibility is on you once the house lights go down to set the tone for the evening. As a general rule, despite the genre, you want to start the set with some energy. This doesn't necessarily mean you can't start with some cool a cappella singing, or other slow-burning intro techniques, but you should follow it up within the first minute or two with something up-tempo.

If you're opening for a national act, your job is to get the crowd warmed up for the headliners. You will usually only have between 30 and 40 minutes to get the energy level of the room up. In these situations, keep the between-song banter to a minimum, and remember to mention to the crowd that the headliners will be up shortly.

Usually, these shows are a great opportunity to showcase your own original music, but if your style is a bit of a departure from the headliners, you may want to consider learning a cover that is in the style of the headlining band (not one of their songs, though, of course). For example, if you are a bluesy band, but the band you're opening for is a grunge band, you may want to learn a popular Pearl Jam or Nirvana tune to throw in to get the crowd excited.

Tip #72: A note on interacting with headliners:

You must remember that, for the most part, these bands will have been on the road for longer than you have. Now, in my experience, the national acts I've toured with have been incredibly gracious and I've even made some friends along the way. I attribute this to the fact that, as a band, we have collectively agreed to give the headliners their space. Some band members like interacting with new people in every city they come to. Those ones will usually come and seek you out. Others prefer to stay on the bus. As someone who doesn't often enjoy mingling with strangers, I completely understand that, too. The bottom line is, you're playing this show because the headliners have either invited or approved you, and you need to show them respect. Even if they're your musical heroes, give them space. This is a job for them (and hopefully for you, too), and part of that job is dealing with fans day in and day out. An apt analogy might be this: If you worked in retail and had to deal with customers all day, would you want your co-workers to act like customers, too?

Tip #73: The P Word

Professionalism is jokingly referred to as "The P Word" around my circle of musician friends. We're all rock musicians, and let's face it, rock musicians don't exactly have a reputation for being steadfast bulwarks of reliability and credibility. Still, the musicians I play with understand that what we do is a job – even if we're not raking in the millions for it – and as such, it deserves nothing less than our absolute best effort. Here are some key aspects of professionalism to remember as you embark on your career as a touring guitarist:

Tip #74: Maintain a Professional Attitude

No matter what kind of day you're having, treat the people involved in the production with dignity, respect, and professionalism. Keep in mind that the success of the show is more important than any personal baggage you're holding onto while getting things set up and even into the performance.

Tip #75: Work Hard in order to Play Hard

This can be taken in a couple of different ways. First, it establishes priorities – work before play – and second it implies that in order to have a great show, a lot of work on the back end needs to be done correctly.

Tip #76: Knowing Your Place/Checking Your Ego

You may be the star of the show, or you may be a hired gun who stands in the background and never gets introduced. In either case, you are a part of a team. Even a solo-acoustic performer needs a staff at the venue to help with the production. You are not the most important thing in the world, and the people you work with – all of them – are just as important to the success of your show as you are.

Recording the Show

A good recording of the show can be very useful in many different ways. For one thing, even if you're the only one who ever hears the recording, you will be able to hear mistakes and sound issues that you can fix on the next show. Think of it as being similar to an athlete watching film of a game afterward in order to see why she missed that catch, or how her form was on the break away. In this way, a recording can be a great tool for improving your performance itself.

One of the other and most obvious ways that recordings of shows can be useful is as promotional tools. Whether it's a live-stream on social media, or a promotional YouTube video, the more ways you can get your fans to hear your music, the better. You can even use live recordings as extra incentives for Patreon or other crowdfunding supporters!

In order to get a good recording of the show, there are a couple of ways to go about it. First, if the sound board has a USB out or some other kind of recording out, you can get what's referred to as a "board recording." The other way is to place a microphone or some other kind of recording decice somewhere out in the venue (usually by the sound desk – but we'll get to that in a minute).

Tip #77: Board Recordings

If you're unfamiliar with board recordings, you're probably going to be disappointed the first time you hear one. With a board recording, you are hearing *exactly* what the mixer is sending to the amplifier and subsequently the speakers. Theoretically, that sounds great, right? Well, consider this. There are guitar amplifiers on stage, and drums that are pretty loud all by themselves too. All of those things are much louder than human vocals. Therefore, the mix you get with a board recording, more often than not, is a whole lot of vocals, and not much instrumentation.

Now, some boards will allow for a more complicated output that will record each channel separately, allowing for a more precise mix later by a professional engineer (or an amateur one).

Tip #78: Portable Recorders

If you want a really good live recording, it's a good idea to invest in a small portable digital recorder. Tascam and Zoom make models with high quality microphones and a lot of features for anywhere from around $100 to $400. The idea is, if you only get a stereo mix from the board, you can place a portable recorder out by the mixing desk. By doing so, the microphones on the portable recorder will pick up what the sound technician – and, theoretically, the audience – is hearing.

A blessing and a curse, these mics will pick up crowd noise. This is a bit of an advantage over a straight board recording if you're planning on releasing the recording, because it will contain the applause between songs. On the other hand, during quieter moments of songs, conversations between audience members will appear on the recording as well.

The ideal situation, then, is to have a board recording with each channel separated out, and a stereo audience mix from a portable recorder, and then give it all to a professional engineer (or you cousin Ray-Bob) to mix together into a fine sounding live recording, suitable for all sorts of promotional and marketing purposes.

Tip #79: Recording Video

Some of today's smartphones have amazing cameras on them that can record dazzling 4K UHD video, and some of them don't. If you're going to do a video, I recommend using a dedicated camera to do so instead of your phone (unless you're just live-streaming to social media). These cameras will ultimately do a better job at capturing the light, and sound (especially if you get one that allows for an external mic input) than your phone will.

Another cool idea I saw one of the national acts I've toured with do was to buy a fairly cheap GoPro camera and send it out into the audience with instructions for them to pass it around for a song or two. Of course, there's the danger that one of the fans will just steal the camera, but it might be worth the risk. I wasn't on the tour with that band long enough to find out if their GoPro got stolen by a fan or not, but I know that for the few dates we played with them, it was a great part of the show.

Working as a Team

In this section I'd like to offer some general advice about how to peacefully and harmoniously interact with your bandmates and anyone else involved with the production. Now, I will not say that I'm an expert in human psychology or relationships, but I've never been "kicked out" of a band, and most of the bands I've been in have lasted for years and even decades. I am not too humble to take at least a little bit of credit for that. If I didn't know how to get along with people, I wouldn't have been able to stay with the bands I've been in for so long.

Tip #80: Maybe it's You

On the other hand, I've known plenty of musicians who have been in and out of so many bands it would make your head spin. These people usually share some common traits:

- They let their egos control their behavior.
- They are inflexible.
- They are unwilling to reflect on their own faults and improve (musically and personally).
- They are flakey and unreliable.
- They are abrasive.

Pro tip/Life hack: If you keep getting kicked out of bands, or if your bands keep breaking up, it's probably not them. Check yourself against the list above.

Tip #81: Know Your Bandmates

There are a lot of sterotypes about musicians out there, and there are even more when you start looking at each specific type of instrumentalist or vocalist. Some of these stereotypes make for great jokes (How do you know if the stage is level? *There's drool coming out of both sides of the drummer's mouth.* Or my personal favorite: What do you call a guitar player without a girlfriend? *Homeless*.), but like all stereotypes, they can be very harmful and completely inaccurate as well. Nevertheless, there are distinct personality types that, in my experience playing with a lot of different groups, tend to gravitate toward certain instruments.

This does **not** mean that all drummers are morons, or that all guitarists are flakes who can't take care of themselves, but it does give us at least a useful place to start when talking about the different personality types you'll likely be dealing with at some point. So we'll talk about each personality type in comparison with the instrument itself, to add metaphorical illustration, not to reinforce stereotypes.

Tip #82: Bass Players

In my experience, there are two different types of bass player out there. There are people who chose to play bass from the beginning, and then there are guitar, piano, or keyboard players who end up playing bass because the band can't find anyone else to do it.

How do you tell the difference? Well, the guy/gal that wanted to be a bass player from the start is most likely not going to be a front-person. I know, you're raving "What about Sting? What about Geddy Lee? What about Lemmy? What about Doug Pinnick?" Well, yes, those are all legendary bass players who also happen to be legendary front men. But look at their playing. For nearly all of them, their playing is very melodic and tends to follow the guitar and keys more than it locks in with the drums. On the other hand, a bass player like John Paul Jones, Jack Bruce, and Tony Levin incorporate melody into their bass playing, but that melody is separate from the melodic instruments and more locked into the rhythm section of the band.

If you have a bona-fide bass player – the one who was born to play bass – he or she will probably have a personality that likes to be the side-person. They like to be the one that still gets to interact with the audience, but who, musically would much rather be the foundation than the panache.

Interacting with Bass Players: When interacting with bass players, remember that they may be more introverted than you, and they may need more time to themselves. Also, in my experience, if a bass player has something to say, it's usually worth listening to, because born bass players choose their notes and their words very carefully.

The other type of bass player will need to be dealt with in the manner suited most to his or her original instrument. God help you if he or she is another lead guitarist.

What Your Bass Player Needs from You:

Regardless of which type of bass player you have, they will need you to be as solid as possible musically. Now, it's part of their job to help keep you in the pocket, but it's a two-way street. Guitar players have a tendency to rush things, rhythmically, so the more aware you can be of your tempo, the easier it will make things on your bass player. Just as important, if not more, is that they need you to keep your prima-donna level in check.

Whether he admits it or not, imagine how Rob Grange, Ted Nugent's bass player on "Stranglehold" feels every time he had to play the exact same four-bar bass riff over and over for ten to twenty minutes while Terrible Ted and his Ten Fingers of Doom wanked on over the top of it with an over-indulgent guitar solo. The guy could have probably written an entire novella in his head every night during that solo. My point is – especially for blues and rock players – have your fun, play a great solo, but keep in mind, that your bass player is holding down the same three or four chords every minute that you're indulging yourself. Be kind. Keep the solos tasteful and not over-indulgent.

Tip #83: Drummers

Buy a drum machine.

Okay, just kidding. On a serious note about the personality type, I have to say that the most diverse range of personalities I've worked with have been in the drummer role. At its core, the position of drummer requires a degree of fitness, of mathematical prowess, of creativity, of swagger, and of groove. You can get those things with a lot of different personality types. Don't forget, though, there's also the fact that drummers get to hit stuff... a lot. That's not insignificant.

Some drummers really are simple when it comes to social skills or emotional intelligence. (This does not mean that they're dumb or anything like that; instead, what I mean is that they don't over-think things.) These personality types are really easy to work with on the whole. As long as the general "vibe" of the show or the rehearsal or the tour is good, then they're good.

Some drummers are the opposite, though. They can be very cerebral and get lost in the intricacies of every beat they play. Neil Peart (for all I know of him, anyway) comes to mind. These personalities tend to be pretty analytical and often are introverted.

Some drummers are nut-cases (that's the technical term). These are the Keith Moons, the John Bonhams, etc. The guys or gals that just want to live the full-on rock and roll lifestyle, and have a blast beating the hell out of their drums each night.

In any of these cases, you'll have to get to know which kind of personality you're dealing with. As with any of the other personalities, each one will be different.

Interacting with Drummers: Buy a drum machine.

Seriously, though, remember that drummers have perhaps the most responsibility in the band. There's nothing that will kill a song quicker than the beat dropping. A singer can forget the words and most of the audience will never know, a guitarist or bass player can miss a note and it won't mess much up, but if the beat drops, **everyone** looks at the drummer. That said, your drummer is probably comfortable with that level of responsibility, which should make him or her a pretty solid person to talk to when you're out on the road.

What Your Drummer Needs From You: Don't drown out the bass player or the vocalists with your amp on stage. Keep your stage volume relatively low – especially if your amp is set up near the drum kit. Again, drummers and bass players need to work very closely together to keep the groove going, and if some idiot flashy guitarist comes along, cranks his amp to eleven, and then starts playing the song one and a half times the normal tempo, it makes it a bit hard for them to do their jobs.

Tip #84: Keyboardists

Keyboardists are very similar to bass players in that there are usually two different types. There is the type of keyboardist who is more comfortable playing piano or organ, and then there's the keyboardist who wants to create ambiance, rhythm, and texture with synth sounds. As with bass players, the personalities often associated with these two camps are very different.

Pianists and organists most have most likely been taking piano lessons since the time they were old enough to reach the pedals. They tend to be fairly, for lack of a better word, "square" personalities that like to add color to the song. Like bass players, they are comfortable being "side men."

Synth players can be a whole different ball of wax. On one hand, you can have someone like Richard Wright, who is only interested in serving the song – even if it means he's the least well-known member of the band, and on the other hand, you can have someone like Keith Emmerson, who will take every opportunity he can to show off his technical prowess and ability to splatter weird noises all over the song. By the way, Ray Manzarek, I'm convinced is more of a synth player than an organist, but synths weren't well-developed enough yet during The Doors' glory days, so he worked with what he had.

Interacting with Keyboardists: Just like with the other instrumental positions, you'll want to get to know your keyboardist's personality before you will really know how to interact with her or him. On the whole, the pianists and organists of the world will be happy to be a part of the fun, whatever that fun is, while the synth players could be a grab-bag (you never know what you're going to get).

What Your Keyboardist Needs from You: This will be similar to what another guitarist would need from you – balance regarding the onstage volume level and balance. Make sure the keyboardist can hear him/herself, and that you aren't being selfish with the solo time. If your keyboardist has the chops, let him or her show 'em off! When they're soloing, hang back.

Turn the volume knob on your guitar down. Play more simply. Let *them* shine.

Tip #85: Vocalists

If you have a member of the band whose only job is to sing... kick him or her out.

Okay, just kidding again. To be more austere, though, singers probably have the worst reputation problem of any of the musician stereotypes. They are often assumed to be prima-donnas, or divas, or just downright egomaniacs. And sometimes, those qualities are definitely there, and those qualities definitely make that lead vocalist one hell of a front person. Neither David Lee Roth, Axl Rose, nor Jim Morrison would have been the bright stars they were without a certain X-factor that is easy to associate with narcissism and abrasive personalities. On the other hand, they all let those qualities become ultimately destructive to the success of their bands.[1]

Then there are vocalists like Mick Jagger, Robert Plant, and Roger Daultrey – all of whom had/have vibrant and larger-than-life public personas but have still managed to be the only vocalists in their

---

[1] Technically, and tragically, Jim Morrison passed away before The Doors broke up, but I contend that with Morrison's both on-and-off-stage antics, The Doors wouldn't have lasted much longer with him at the helm – especially considering the fates of the other frontmen and bands I mentioned.

legendary bands. Despite well-documented problems within each band, in all three cases, the vocalists have allowed their professionalism to triumph over their egos in order to make some fantastic music over decades.

Regardless of the size or handling of your lead-vocalist's ego, however, the good ones work their asses off. To quote the fictional Jeff Bebe (played masterfully by Jason Lee in Cameron Crowe's *Almost Famous*), "I work *as* hard, if not *harder* than anyone on that stage! You know what I do? I make people get off! I find the one guy in the audience who's not getting off, and I *MAKE* him get off!"[2] It really is a lot of work connecting with an audience, and that, above all else is the front-person's job.

How to Deal with Vocalists: The way I see it, you have three options: First, you can learn to sing and take the front-person job for yourself. Second, you can insist that your current vocal-only front-person learn an instrument for themselves so that they have to do some real work; and third, you can work with your current front-person on how to communicate and cooperate effectively with the rest of the band.

Alright, alright. Those aren't your only options, though they are all valid in their own way - the part about real work was a joke, though. As I mentioned above, the job of a great front-person takes a lot of guts, a lot of energy, and a lot of work. Make sure that

---

2 Crowe, Cameron, writer/director. *Almost Famous*. Columbia Pictures, 2000.

that work is appreciated, and you should be able to get along with a vocalist just fine.

What Your Vocalist Needs from You: Play your parts correctly. Many vocalists really count on cues from the guitarists to start verses, choruses, and bridges. If you don't play key elements of a song at the right time, a whole vocal performance can be thrown off. Also try not to upstage them.

Tip #86: Sound Technicians

If you have a good sound tech, you'd better treat him or her like a god(dess) among mortals. If you have an imbecile, then buckle up, because your show's going to be a bumpy ride.

A good sound technician is a student of acoustics and audio signal processing. She knows her gear in and out, and she knows how to tune a room to make the smallest, most ill-designed club space sound like an opera house.

An imbecile is a guy that shows up because his cousin owns the bar. He used to run the sound board in drama class in high school and now cousin Earl pays him $50 a night to make sure the speakers don't make the squealy noise.

How to Deal with Sound Technicians: First, let me reiterate. Good sound person? Treat her as divinity. Do exactly as she says, and have a great show. Just worry about playing and connecting with your audience. Imbecile? Buckle up. You can try to get something out of him, but you may just end up causing more problems than it's worth. In this situation, you'll just have to power through. Be professional, though. **Never** berate an imbecile from the stage, and preferably never at all. It will only succeed in making you look like a jerk. Instead, be polite and play the best show you can. Tomorrow's another night, and hopefully you'll have Athena at the sound board instead of Gomer Pyle.

What Your Sound Technician Needs from You: Patience and professionalism, first of all, and a good helping of praise for a proper sound tech wouldn't kill you either. If you have a good tech, follow all of her instructions and trust her. If she says turn your amp down, your answer had better be "How much?"

Tip #87: Playing with Visiting Musicians

Every so often, a show gets put together where the bands on the bill really get on with one another, and crazy things ensue. I've been in these situations multiple times. I've played songs I've never played before onstage with guitarists from the national bands for whom I was opening, and I've sang and played a cover of a Rock-and-Roll-Hall-of-Famer's song while he tweeted video of the charade from the side of the stage. Crazy things can happen on the road – embrace the strange!

The key to making these impromptu performances – when the totally amazing accordion player whose house you crashed in the night before agrees to join you on stage for that show and he's only just heard your song for the first time five minutes ago – is active listening. You absolutely must be sensitive to what *all* of the other players onstage are doing and be able to adjust at a moment's notice. When all else fails, fall back (unless you're the one driving the song – in that case, just plow through!).

Chapter 6: Merchandise and Revenue

Of course, a major part of the reason most of us do these insane tours is because they are a blast and they are an experience unlike any other we will ever have. On the other hand, traveling around and playing in clubs isn't cheap, and it's definitely not free. As we discussed in the planning chapter, you need to have a good budget laid out, and you need to figure out how you're going to cover the expenses of the tour. Generally, there are a couple of ways of generating revenue when you are on the road. Of course, there's any agreement you may have made with the club owner or promoter about a guarantee, but many small-time bands don't always get that luxury. A more common arrangement is the system by which you get paid a percentage of the cover charge, or of the alcohol sales for the evening. There is also crowdfunding, but if it's done correctly, merch can be a real godsend in the revenue department. In this chapter we'll discuss all of these options.

Merchandise

As mentioned, a well-thought-out merch strategy can be a real game changer. Just look at what George Lucas was able to do with *Star Wars* all because he was savvy enough to secure the merchandising rights from 20th Century Fox up front. Now, you're probably not going to create a $4 billion empire out of your merch business the way Lucas did, but you can definitely do some creative things with merchandise. We'll look at some of them now.

Tip #88: Common Types of Merch

Records: There's some debate out there in the musician community over whether or not CDs are worth pressing any more. In my experience, they are, but my band's demographic is the generation that grew up on CDs. Many bands now save the money on CD manufacturing and just get download cards made up. Download cards are basically business cards with a download redemption code or a QR code printed on them that links directly to a download of your album. Because they don't cost as much as CDs to produce, you can print a ton of them and sell them at a discount at shows.

The strategy there is that if a digital copy your album normally sells for $9.99 on iTunes or Amazon, you can sell the download codes for $5 at shows as an incentive for people to attend shows and for new fans to check out your online presence and other offerings.

Then, of course, there's vinyl. I'm a big fan of getting your album pressed onto vinyl because it crosses the generational gap. If you sell a vinyl copy of your album for $20-$30 and give away a download card with it, this appeals to both generations of music buyers – digital natives and immigrants alike. It's also like a piece of tangible art. You can display a 12" album cover on your wall as artwork; it's harder to do that with a 5" CD liner.

No matter which format you choose, or even if you decide to go with all three, **having recorded copies of your music available at your shows is a must.**

T-Shirts: It seems like one thing bands often overlook is having a selection of t-shirts. Often, it's a matter of budget – you can only afford one design, etc. - but sometimes it's just that the band is not savvy enough about marketing to realize that a reasonable selection conveys a sense of legitimacy and entices potential customers. If you see a show with three bands, the headliner's merch booth probably has at least five to seven different shirt styles available and a handy supply of all sizes. If one of the openers has three different shirt styles and a good selection of sizes, while the other opener only has one fairly simple t-shirt and they're out of a few sizes, most customers will go toward the band that looks more established. Investing in a decent selection and supply of shirts prior tour is a must if you can afford it.

Hats: Sometimes hats can be a good idea, but you don't want cheap ones. If you find a good deal on quality hats (embroidered and well crafted), it may be worth the investment, but it's got to be a really great design and a good price point.

Stickers: You'll end up giving more of these away than selling them, so don't spend too much on them.

Tip #89: Logistics

Unfortunately, somebody's got to man the merch booth. As mentioned in earlier chapters, if you can find one person in the band who actually likes doing this, then, by all means let that person have at it. If not, though, you need to work out a fair schedule of who is going to man the merch booth on which nights.

Typically, if you're an opener, you won't need to man the merch booth throughout the headliner's set. Some traffic will pass by, but those people are usually just going to the bathroom or to buy another drink. Most of the business gets done in between sets, so the best option, really is to just be disciplined as a band and all gather around the merch booth in between sets.

Tip #90: Sales and Marketing

This is going to sound a bit shark-ish, but if you've just played a killer set and there's a line at your merch booth, make *no* deals. Full price for everything. Get as much money from your merch as you can, because you're going to need it down the road. On the other hand, if there's only one or two people hanging out, but they really dug your set, cut 'em a break. Maybe instead of $20 a piece for t-shirts, you give them a buy-two-get-one-free deal. The point is, remember that your music and your merch is valuable (you paid for it, didn't you?). You need to get some of that money back if you want to keep making the music that makes both you and your fans happy.

Crowdfunding

The smart way to go about financing a tour is to get your fans to pay for it in advance via a great crowdfunding campaign. It is, of course, by now means a fool proof way to make enough money to fund your tour, but it certainly helps if you have a reserve of money set up before you set off on your tour.

Tip #91: Types of Crowdfunding Sites

There are a few different types of crowdfunding sites. On some sites you set a goal for your project – for example, $5000 for a tour budget. You offer incentives to your fans to donate to your project – things like special interviews, merchandise, and exclusive perks they can't get any other way than by donating – at different levels. If you don't hit your goal in the time established for the campaign, though, you don't get any of the money you raised, and it all goes back to the contributors.

Some other sites work basically the same way, but they removed the goal restriction, so you get your raised funds whether you reach your goal or not. The big difference here is that for people who donate, they're more likely to see the project they're trying to fund succeed if the goal restrictions are in place. After all, if I donate $100 to see a new season of Firefly get made, then it doesn't ever get made because the goal was never reached, I'd definitely want my money back.

If you're not sure if you can fund your tour without crowdfunding support, then the first model might be more successful for you, because investors will be more attracted to the lower risk if the goal isn't reached.

On the other hand, if you know you're doing the tour whether or not your crowdfunding goal is reached, the non-goal-restricted sites might be a better option, because they give you the opportunity to add unique perks and earn extra money for the tour before it even starts.

Another model is the patron model. In this model, patrons subscribe to your content with the idea that you will provide them with a consistent stream of that content. It's most common with podcasts and other subscription feeds, but musicians who are prolific at writing and recording use these sites too and offer new content on a regular basis.

Tip #92: Perks and Rewards

When choosing the perks and rewards for your crowdfunding campaign, make sure you are offering items or experiences that are one of a kind and that the consumer can only get by donating to your campaign. Personalized signed items (set lists, drum heads, album covers, photos, etc.) are a great idea, as are experiences like private house concerts (for higher donation levels, of course).

Payment

Tip #93: Getting Paid

Aside from merch and crowdfunding revenue, you should, of course, be getting paid from the venue as well. As mentioned above, if you haven't negotiated a guarantee, then you should be getting paid either a percentage of the door or a percentage of the bar-take. With clubs, you will usually be getting cash at the end of the night, however on the odd occasion, a club owner will want to pay with a check.

Which brings me to festivals and other large organized events in which there are official budgets and committees involved. These shows will almost always pay you with a check. There are a couple of different ways to handle this. First, if you are getting a lot of shows and regularly bringing in "band" income, it may be a good idea to set up business checking account with your band's name as the dba. This eliminates confusion when organizers who are none the wiser makes out a check to the Flying Chicken Monkeys from Saturn, instead of you, the band manager. Trust me, the bank will not deposit or cash a check made out to the Flying Chicken Monkeys from Saturn if that's not the name on both your driver's license and bank account.

An easier way to deal with these situations is to stipulate up front to whom the check should be made out. If you're working with a contract for a large festival – make sure it's in the contract. If you're just booking via – e-mail with Tanya, the brewery-owner's wife, make sure you write to her in big, bold letters, that the check is to be made out to you personally.

Tip #94: Managing Band Finances

Another note on payment – the IRS considers what we do (especially if we are getting paid for it) to be a legitimate job in which we are making legitimate income. As such, they expect you to report every dollar you earn – especially if playing guitar is your sole occupation. It may be worth it to set up that dba bank account, and invest in some home-business bookkeeping software to track all of the band's income and expenses.

If you do things this way, it will be easy to set up each band member in your accounting system, assign them a percentage of the total revenue as a paycheck, and it also goes miles toward insuring transparency.

One other handy tip is to divide an extra share. In my band, for example, we only have four members, but we split each show's revenue five ways, with a fifth going toward a general band fund that gets used for emergencies and to fund other projects. I've talked to a lot of other musicians over the years who do things the same way.

Chapter 7: Connecting with Fans and other Bands

Zombies!?! No, Wait. Those Are Your Fans.

Most of us have been to a couple of different kinds of show. In one type of show, the audience is up on its feet, clapping and dancing along, pressed up against the stage, and can't get enough of the band they're seeing. During the other type of show, the fans either stand or sit far away from the stage, faces glued to their phone screens, and it feels like it doesn't matter if you're onstage or not. In both cases, fans can looseley – and cheekily – be compared to zombie hordes. I do not mean this disparagingly, only to illustrate that concert-going crowds are subject to huge social-psychological forces, and you want to be careful what kind of zombies (fans) you get. So how do we get scenario-one zombies (fans) - the fast kind like those in *World War Z* or *28 Days Later*, and not scenario-two zombies (fans) - the slow moving, bumbling hordes from *Night of the Living Dead* or *The Walking Dead*?

Tip #95: How to Keep the Crowd Engaged

Well, first, acknowledge them. Remember the anecdote about Eric Johnson I mentioned earlier? Now, I love EJ's music, but I doubt I'd ever shell out the cash to see him live again if he were the headliner, just because I'd expect to see not more than a brilliantly talented guitar virtuoso in his own world with his headphone monitors on, seemingly oblivious to the fact that there are even other people in the room. On the other hand, even though I'm less a fan of his music, I'd probably pay to see Satriani again, because he interacted with the crowd the entire set.

It's cool to start a set out with two or three back to back songs to keep that energy level up for ten or fifteen minutes straight, but audiences need a bit of a break after that. Build time into your set to talk to the audience – and not just all of them as a whole. You can take some time to make individual audience members feel special, too. Reach out and give them a fist bump – or, if you're feeling really adventurous – bring them up on stage to sing with you. (I try to avoid this anymore, however, because it never ends up being a good song, just a good gimmick.) The bottom line: never forget that there is a crowd of people all anxious to have a good time and expecting you to give it to them. Saddle up and get to work.

Tip #96: Connecting with Fans After the Show

Make sure that at your merch booth you have some way to get contact info from your fans. Whether it's an e-mail list, or simply a QR code that sends their smart-phone to your social media sites so that they can connect instantly, you want a system in place so that if a fan hears you in Salt Lake City for the first time, he or she can easily follow you on social media and get updates the next time you're in Utah.

Occasionally you'll have fans that will come up to you and want to dominate your time after the show. You need to be cordial and polite here, but if there are other fans waiting for your attention or to give you money for merch, kindly move them along so that you can conduct the rest of your business. If they're really that interested in talking to you about how awesome your cover of "Folsom Prison Blues" was and telling you all about how their grandpa's dog used to howl during the guitar solos, then they'll wait until the rest of the fans have had their turns with their transactions and interactions.

Keep in mind that many fans – especially after the show – will be inebriated to some degree, so you have to be prepared for that. Remember that their "impaired" state is probably affecting their personalities, so try not to be too judgmental. Again, be polite and cordial, even if the fans are out of line. Use security if necessary, but for the most part, if you just keep calm and remember that meeting interesting people on the road is half the fun, you shouldn't run into any altercations unless someone is just looking ot cause trouble.

Above all, remember that if there are no fans, there is no show. Treat your fans with respect and take every opportunity to connect with them. After all, for most of them, you're something of a wizard –being able to make wonderful sounds with equipment that the majority of people don't understand. It's natural for them to want to connect with you, and the least you can do is give them a few moments.

Tip #97: Retaining Fans After the Show

As mentioned above, there are a lot of ways in this age of social media and global connection to stay involved with your fans long after you've left their city. In the old days, it was a mailing list, or an official fan club with a monthly newsletter. Then, in the '90s, e-mail lists became popular, and those same newsletter updates were sent electronically. As of about ten years ago, everything has started to move to social media – especially for musicians. The contemporary age of social media offers bands and content creators of all stripes to constantly engage their fanbase. In fact, some of the WordPress blogs I follow post up to ten blogs a day! That's an insane amount of clamoring for attention, and a lot of media clutter to cut through if you're trying to compete for the attention of your fan base.

Based on my experience, here are some general pointers for staying connected:

- You need to post regularly to ensure that your posts show up in your fans' news feeds, but – even though there is some debate among the experts about this – I'm of the mind that it still needs to be quality content. Those bloggers I mentioned who post double-digit blogs per day? I never read a single one. There's just too much there, and the only thing those bloggers are really accomplishing by posting so much are a.) I know their names. b.) I associate those names with annoying notifications about ten blog posts a day. Now, I'm no marketing expert, but I don't want my fans to have _any_ negative associations with my band, so I prefer to keep the posts regular and relevant.

- Contests, polls, and other such strategies are often a great way to keep your audience engaged, as well.
- Find a social media platform that works well for you and **own** it. If you notice that you have more Instagram followers than Facebook likes, then focus on Instagram. Really build up that base, and then use that platform to grow all of the others.

Working with Other Bands on the Road

If you plan on touring around your region a lot, it's a good idea to make friends with other bands along the way. These connections will help you book return visits to cities in which you might not otherwise have had a foot in the door. Plus, other bands are usually a lot of fun, so take some time and get to know the other bands on your bill.

Tip #98: Show-Swapping

One of the most common ways for bands to help each other out is to do show-swaps. The idea here is, one band has a show booked in their city that needs another band, and they ask you to fill the slot with the understanding that the next time you have an open slot while putting together a show in your hometown, you'll put them on it. It's a great way to build those relationships and your bands' respective fanbases.

Tip #99: Cross-Promotion

If you are putting on a show with several other bands, and you know them, you may want to coordinate and even pool resources when it comes to promotion. Get creative. There are many different ways to get fans involved, especially when there are two or more bands hustling for it. Just for an example, your two bands might decide to do a special poll where they let the audience decide a cover song that they'll perform together at the show, or a dual-band merch and music giveaway contest through social media. The sky's the limit when you learn to cooperate rather than compete.

Tip #100: Cost-Sharing

This doesn't happen as much in my experience, but it is an option. If two bands from the same town are both looking to do a tour, it may be more cost effective for them to join forces, travel together in a single, bigger rig. Doing a two-band tour will definitely take more work, but it won't necessarily be twice as much work, and the rewards could be really satisfying for everyone involved.

Tip #101: A Final Thought on Connecting

Like I said earlier, the audience – your fans (faithful and potential alike) - are the most important part of any show. In my bands, when there's a low turnout at a show where we have a guarantee, we often joke that it's basically a paid rehearsal. However, though it makes for a decent joke, it never really makes for a decent show. The best you can do is connect with the people who *are* there. Maybe one or two of the people who see you – even at a show with only twelve people in the audience – will be really moved by what they see and hear and become your biggest fans, championing you and your music to everyone they know both in real life and across the digital realm. Even though touring can sometimes be a slog, the people who paid to see you are there to have a good time, and it's your job to give it to them.

Epilogue

Though you won't find me on the cover of Rolling Stone any time soon, and I won't be attending any Grammy celebrations this year, next year, or probably ever, I wouldn't trade the life I've lived as a guitar player for anything. Despite being financially undervalued, and despite the grind of loading and unloading, dealing with drunks, promoters, and just plain weirdos, and the outright boredom of a third seven-hour travel day in a row, the feeling I get when I get on stage and play the first note makes it all worth it.

Though the scope of this book was more broad than deep, I hope that you've found some tips and information here that will make your own experience on the road much more smooth and enjoyable – for both you and your fans.

Please keep in mind that new information about gear is constantly evolving, and that there may be many other shortcuts and hacks made possible by new gear and new tech, so keep your eyes open for new innovations and how you might be able to use them to make both your music and your performance better.

Above all else, we do this job because it makes people – our audience *and* ourselves – happy. Though our job sounds easy, as you've hopefully seen from this book, there's a lot of planning and work that goes into putting on a successful show, let alone a successful string of them in the form of a tour. Touring and playing music for people is one of the most fulfilling things a person can do with his or her time, and if you plan properly, practice persistently, and perform professionally, you will have a great show nearly every time!

Good luck out there!

About the Expert

Brandon Humphreys has been playing guitar and singing in semi-professional and tour-support bands for over twenty years. He has played music across the Western United States and Canada, often in support of national acts. Across his various bands, he has recorded and released four full-length albums and two EPs. He has also appeared as a session guitarist for other artists. As a performer, he has "sat-in" with countless groups at countless performances over the years and has lent his talents to rock, jazz, blues, country, and big bands.

When not playing music, Brandon is a writer and a professional educator.

HowExpert publishes quick 'how to' guides on unique topics by everyday experts. Visit HowExpert.com to learn more.

Recommended Resources

www.HowExpert.com – Quick 'How To' Guides on Unique Topics by Everyday Experts.

www.HowExpert.com/writers - Write About Your #1 Passion/Knowledge/Experience.

www.HowExpert.com/membership - Learn a New 'How To' Topic About Practically Everything Every Week.

www.HowExpert.com/jobs - Check Out HowExpert Jobs.

Made in the USA
Middletown, DE
02 December 2019